THE J   'NT

The Idiom of Dissent

Edited by
T. Robin Chapman

Gomer

Published in 2006 by
Gomer Press, Llandysul, Ceredigion SA44 4JL
www.gomer.co.uk

ISBN 1 84323 590 0
ISBN-13 9781843236903
A CIP record for this title is available from the British Library

This book is published with the financial support of the
Welsh Books Council.

Printed and bound in Wales at
Gomer Press, Llandysul, Ceredigion

CONTENTS

FOREWORD BY DAFYDD ELIS-THOMAS   vii

PREFACE   ix

WOMEN VERSUS 'THE PEOPLE': LANGUAGE, NATION AND
   CITIZENSHIP, 1906–11
   Ursula Masson   1

THEISM'S LAST HURRAH: SAUNDERS LEWIS'S CAERNARFON
   COURT SPEECH OF 1936
   T. Robin Chapman   24

WALDO WILLIAMS, 'IN TWO FIELDS', AND THE 38TH PARALLEL
   Damian Walford Davies   43

FRAMING WALES: THE PARLIAMENT FOR WALES CAMPAIGN,
   1950–1956
   Emily Charette   75

GREENHAM AND ITS LEGACY – THE WOMEN'S PEACE
   MOVEMENT IN WALES IN THE 1980S
   Avril Rolph   97

DEVOLUTION: A VIEW FROM THE RIGHT
   Nick Bourne   123

THE IDIOMS OF RACE: THE 'RACIST NATIONALIST' IN WALES
   AS BOGEYMAN
   Simon Brooks   139

NOTES ON CONTRIBUTORS   166

FOREWORD

It was Professor Gwyn Alf Williams who once wondered what it would be like to belong to a nation that didn't have to shout at the top of its voice to remind itself that it still exists.

But such strident assertion of identity has often manifested itself in campaigns on altogether different matters, especially those campaigns where there has been a strong appeal to natural justice in the face of establishment apathy, derision, suppression or oppression.

This diverse and entertaining collection of essays, featuring some of our most incisive cultural commentators and some unlikely cohabitees), pays particular attention to the language used by the protestors of twentieth and twenty-first-century Wales in their onslaught on the status quo and their promotion of their ideas and ideals. A number of the writers also focus on the language of counter-protest, seeking to illustrate how the authorities and the media have chosen to represent and respond to those outspoken and dissenting voices.

As a late convert to the need for a Welsh 'establishment', I am also determinedly proud of its 'radical' and 'rebellious' tradition, and of the sophisticated and memorable ways in which this has been expressed. And now we have 'become' a political nation, our democracy can only thrive on dissent. Let's continue, therefore, to celebrate the political, religious, moral and cultural diversity that is the natural (and welcome) result of such dissent, especially where we disagree with its positions!

DAFYDD ELIS-THOMAS
Presiding Officer of the National Assembly for Wales

PREFACE

Twentieth-century Wales was an uppity place. The aim of this collection is to ask how that uppitiness – cultural, religious, moral and political – has expressed itself.

In the essays that follow – presented in broadly chronological order and spilling over into the twenty-first century – the contributors have interpreted the brief they were given in the broadest conceivable way. Ursula Masson's essay reminds us that language can be both a bridge and a wall. Her revelation of a less-than-liberal side to Welsh Liberalism at the turn of the century adds a valuable chapter to the seemingly inexhaustible narrative of Lloyd George's life. My own piece discusses a very different Welsh icon. This analysis of Saunders Lewis's Caernarfon court speech may suggest why a nationalist party founded and led by writers and artists could create a cultural landmark but fail so signally to win popular support.

In his study, Damian Walford Davies offers another figure in a landscape. His close parallel reading of the contesting voices who have sought to translate Waldo Williams's most famous poem into an English idiom offers insights into the nature of protest as cultural practice and locates a poet often seen as a voice of universal brotherhood firmly in the 1950s. The 1950s is also the setting for Emily Charette's narrative of missed opportunities and mixed messages that was the Parliament for Wales Campaign. Her use of the notion of 'framing' is a model of how to read the protest of persuasion.

Avril Rolph brings the story of protest into the 1980s. Her account of the Welsh feminist dimensions of anti-nuclear protest, together with previously unpublished evidence from those involved, serves as a useful reminder of an era when Wales embraced identity politics as its own industrial identity crumbled. Nick Bourne AM, from a diametrically opposed political tradition to Avril Rolph, traces how the Conservative party in Wales learned to love devolution a decade later. His inside story reminds us that Welsh politics is never dull. Simon Brooks rounds off the century with a passionate and closely-argued piece on what happens when principle is reflected by the popular and new media through the distorting mirror of two languages and two sets of cultural assumptions.

It has been my pleasure to work with six writers from widely different backgrounds and with different values. They often disagree with each other and I with them, and the opinions they express are entirely their own. That said, all of them would, I hope, concur with four views of what protest is and does. The first is that protest throws culture into relief: it challenges consensus and calls what was acceptable suddenly into question. It obliges culture to explain itself. Second, the discourse of protest, because of the context in which it inevitably occurs or the reaction which it inexorably provokes, is unnatural language for unnatural times; it is language *in extremis*, vulnerable, accusatorial, savage, simultaneously mannered and emotional. Third, protest takes a brass-rubbing of culture: it can make clear on paper what cannot always be seen clearly in the fabric of culture itself, by highlighting the raised letters on its surface. And fourth, protest itself makes cultural choices. When a protestor uses the discourse of health and sickness, encroachment, or battle, he or she does so, consciously or unconsciously, in the same way that a writer uses language. Protest is never just an act, in either sense of the word.

This can only ever be an introduction (and an incomplete one at that) to the language of protest in twentieth-century Wales. The National Strike, Tryweryn, language protests and the miners' dispute of the mid 1980s, for instance, all await a historian who can assess the rhetoric that shaped them. However, these essays will, I hope, make the contentious Wales of the twentieth century less of a foreign country.

I would like to thank Ceri Wyn Jones for steering this through from initial idea to finished product. Diolch yn fawr am bopeth.

T. ROBIN CHAPMAN

WOMEN VERSUS 'THE PEOPLE': LANGUAGE, NATION AND CITIZENSHIP 1906–11

Ursula Masson

. . . the full representation of the people is a Liberal principle, and cannot be considered to be accomplished as long as more than half the population is without a vote.[1]

Men were not 'the people', men and women together were 'the people'. . . . It was a farce, and the sooner men talked less of the will of the people the better.[2]

Introduction

Languages of belonging, inclusiveness and self-assertion are also languages of exclusion and alienation. The beginning of the twentieth century saw the revival of a traditional Liberal language of populism and nationhood in a way which sought to silence women's demands for an inclusive citizenship. The context was the deteriorating relationship between women and Liberalism from 1906–11. While claiming their support in its confrontation with the House of Lords, the Liberal Party did its best to silence women's claims for representation in the nation. The effect was increasingly to delegitimize, suffragists protested, the participation of women in the public political sphere. In this process, concepts of 'decency', of 'freedom of speech', of localism, and of Welshness were used both against and in defence of the suffragists.

Above all, during the constitutional crisis of 1909–10 the

language of government ministers and supporters, including the Liberal press, became increasingly populist, as they conjured up the 'coming battle between the Peers and the People'. Language traditionally used in oppositional discourses by radicals and reformers, to claim a wider citizenship and a voice for the unenfranchised, was now being used in support of government policy – albeit radical policy – in a way which attempted to silence and exclude half the population. There was a specifically Welsh dimension to the use of this dual language of inclusivity and exclusion, injected by the central role in events of David Lloyd George, the Chancellor of the Exchequer. In addition to the meanings of 'the People' traditionally expressed in British radical discourses, Lloyd George was able to extend the concept by drawing on the understanding of 'the people of Wales' formulated by Henry Richard in the 1860s, and nurtured in Cymru Fydd, the Welsh Liberal National movement at the end of the century.

The relationship of women to populist language, and representations of national identity, had always been problematic,[3] but in the Cymru Fydd period, Liberal women had made determined, and partly successful, efforts to reshape the masculinist language of nationalism, and ensure the inclusion of women. Support for women's political and social aims, represented as 'rights and duties', had become integral to Liberal visions for Wales.[4] However, feminists and suffragists continued to have an awkward relationship with 'Welshness', most fully explored by Angela V. John,[5] who has examined how, in the Edwardian period, '[n]ationality, language, history and a claim to the proverbial high moral ground were drawn upon to distance suffragettes from the true Welsh'.[6] John has explored issues of masculinity and the disruption of gender relations, in response to 'the transgressive nature of [militant] female activists', and, briefly, the Lloyd George 'factor' as an issue for Welsh supporters of women's suffrage, in a period when the Chancellor was a member of a Liberal cabinet with other priorities.[7] In the constitutional showdown which started when the Lords rejected the re-distributive 1909 budget – the People's Budget – the overriding priority for Liberals was the passage of the Parliament Act, which would curb the vetoing power of the House of Lords. This in turn would enable the achievement of the rest of the government's legislative programme including National Insurance, Home Rule for Ireland, and Welsh Church disestablishment.

The other crisis, inextricable from these political factors, was in the suffrage movement. It had become clear that a Liberal government under Asquith would not introduce a women's suffrage bill. The resulting escalation of suffragist militancy is well known; constitutional suffragists within and outside the Liberal Party also became increasingly disaffected, leading to a haemorrhage of women from the party.[8] Cardiff supplies a vivid case-study of the process. From 1906, the loyalty of the Cardiff Women's Liberal Association, and their electoral work-horse skills, were outrageously exploited and betrayed by the MP (Ivor Guest 1906–09) and by the constituency party. The split in the local party forces came in the middle of the crucial December 1910 election campaign, leading to the loss of the seat to the Unionists. It signalled a fatal division of the forces of local women's Liberalism, and the creation of a large and influential suffrage society. In the process, the last remains of the old Welsh radicalism, now reduced to the single demand for disestablishment, were abandoned by a significant body of women.

Cardiff Women Liberals: Out of 'villadom'

Cardiff Women's Liberal Association (WLA) was formed in 1890. It had its roots in the Nonconformist activism of the town, connected to the earliest suffrage organisation, to the campaign to repeal the Contagious Diseases Acts, to the temperance movement, and to the men's Liberal Association through family politics. In the early 1890s, after visiting organisers judged it too confined to 'villadom', it had a number of re-launches, expanding into a city-wide society with a membership, a decade later, of over one thousand. It retained its woman-centred moral-reform aspect into the twentieth century, but also developed in a Progressive and New Liberal direction through involvement in local government, particularly the Board of Guardians, and in cooperation with

women from a wide spectrum of social activism in the city,
including Labour movement women. Its subscribers, if not active
members, now represented a broader swathe of the social base of
the city, including working-class women, and many teachers,
academics and other educated professional women created by the
expansion of intermediate and higher education of the 1890s, and
drawn to the opportunities of the burgeoning university town. This
expansion brought into the association women who may not have
been primarily committed to the old Nonconformist agenda which
dominated the town's politics up to the First World War, creating a
coalition with fault-lines which were to prove vulnerable to the
stresses of Edwardian politics. The demoralization of a long period
in opposition for the Liberals, 1896–1906, and the divisions
caused by the Second Anglo-Boer War, against which the
Women's Liberal Federation (WLF) had provided a core of
opposition,[9] weakened local organization. Cardiff WLA remained
a large society, however. It was invaluable in election campaigns
and should have been able to exercise influence in Cardiff
Liberalism – in the choice of candidates, for example. The
destructive impact of the suffrage issue after 1906 is therefore all
the more evident as the coalition of interests and identities, built
up over twenty years, was rapidly dismantled.[10]

The Liberal candidate in the 1906 general election was Ivor
Guest, a former Unionist who had crossed the floor to support
Liberal free-trade policies. Guest was a known opponent of
women's suffrage;[11] his family had developed an anti-suffrage
tradition, and his mother, Lady Wimborne, a founder of the
Ladies' Grand Council of the Primrose League, had been one of
the signatories of the notorious 1889 Appeal Against Female
Suffrage. Guest needed the WLA to work for his election, so the
association was able to extract a pledge from him that he would
not oppose women's suffrage, and two hundred women worked to
get him elected. They soon had cause to regret their efforts: while
technically honouring his pledge by abstaining from voting on
women's suffrage in the Commons, Guest intervened in the second
reading debate on the Women's Franchise Bill of February 1908 to
warn of 'the serious menace which would be the result if women
had the vote'. Thereafter, as anti-suffragism entered its organised

and active phase, Guest took a prominent role, first as secretary, then treasurer, to the Women's National Anti-Suffrage League, formed in the summer of 1908.[12] The demoralization of at least a section of the association must have been significant, the extent to which their loyalty had been abused being all too clear; these members now began to turn to alternative methods of pursuing their suffrage aims. The formation of the Cardiff and District Women's Suffrage Society (C&DWSS) was announced in July; while the president of the new society was a Tory, Liberal domination of the new society was clear among the names of the executive committee, which included WLA president Edith Lester Jones.[13]

Decency and indecency in the political sphere

Many of the political events in Cardiff and South Wales more generally in this period can be understood in terms of the 'politics of disruption', suffragettes' attempts to disrupt male control of the political sphere and public space, and Liberal and masculinist counter-attack.[14] The Women's Social and Political Union (WSPU) had, since 1905, developed the tactic of disrupting political meetings addressed by ministers, including continuous interruption, which meant that speeches might go completely unheard, or meetings be abandoned.[15] This gave rise to a number of responses, at the level of government and local party. The rank-and-file of young men in the party – their numbers swollen by other opponents of women's suffrage, and by freelance hooligans – turned the tables (as they saw it) on the suffragists by breaking up their meetings, drowning out speeches, in some cases creating near-riot conditions. As a prominent member of the Liberal Cabinet against which the WSPU was waging war, Lloyd George was the frequent target of disruption, inside and outside Wales. Following his experience when speaking in support of women's suffrage, at the Albert Hall meeting of 5 December 1908, Lloyd George announced 'reluctantly' that he would address no more meetings at which women were present, and a private bill criminalizing conduct which prevented the business of a public meeting, and sanctioning the use of private stewards to keep order, was quickly passed into law. Liberal Party organisations and national leadership attempted to prevent women from attending political meetings where ministers were speaking, or forbade them from asking questions. The ticketing of meetings was made tighter, creating, as the C&DWSS put it, 'humiliating' conditions on women's entry. There was no attempt in any of this to distinguish between militant and constitutionalist suffragists, or between Liberal and non-party women. Indeed, the militant speakers who toured South Wales at this time, holding meetings on street corners and at factory or dock gates, got off much more lightly from the impromptu crowds which gathered – mainly of young boys and working men – than did suffragists at the indoor meetings subject to organized wrecking by Liberal supporters.[16]

In South Wales, the most vivid examples of the 'politics of disruption', containing very real threats of violence and bodily harm, were provided by male Liberals and anti-suffragists. In 1908, meetings in Cardiff, Pontypridd, and Caldicot, organized by Liberal women and members of local branches of the Women's Freedom League (WFL), were to be addressed by National Union of Women's Suffrage Societies (NUWSS) president, Millicent Fawcett, and WFL president Charlotte Despard, with platforms arranged to represent local male Liberal support.[17] Despard, a long-time socialist, also spoke at Llanelli and Swansea for the ILP. The meetings were broken up, and women were driven from the meeting halls and hunted through the streets with a ferocity which requires explanation. It is clear that the demonstrators were government supporters from the interpretation of the crowd's behaviour as 'paying back in their own coin' those who disrupted meetings of cabinet ministers.[18] However, the organizers and speakers at these events were themselves wholly innocent of the disruptive tactics against government ministers being imitated, as it was claimed, by the crowd.[19] An explanation for the Liberal Party's 'extraordinarily hostile reaction' to the WSPU can be extended to the reaction to suffragists more generally.[20] Since 1902, the WLF had withheld electoral assistance from Liberal opponents of women's suffrage, though allowing local associations to decide their own policy. After making 'massive efforts' in support of the failed February 1908 Women's Suffrage Bill, some members of the WLF executive committee had resigned, and were to be found sharing platforms with the militants,[21] while around the country WLA members resigned from their associations to join suffrage societies. The Liberal Party and its supporters vented their anger and embarrassment at the pressure from Liberal women, their 'own' women, their 'natural' supporters on the side of reform, and irreplaceable election workers. Millicent Fawcett, president of the largest suffrage organisation, as a Liberal Unionist, and one who had moved increasingly towards Conservatism (although in this period supporting free trade), might particularly have been perceived as embodying this dangerous apostasy, traitorously supported by local Liberal men.

The incidents reveal the contest for occupancy of political spaces and representation in the life of the nation and the locality; a contest not, as was customary in local political life, of parties or factions, but of gender.[22] By force of numbers, volume of noise, and the threat of violence – sheer, massed maleness – the suffragists were denied a hearing. Just how effectively they were denied a hearing is evident from the Pontypridd meeting at which communication from the platform was reduced to two placards held up to plead 'Give Mrs. Fawcett one minute', and to announce the end of the meeting.[23] Their spaces within the halls were invaded and occupied, as were the open spaces of the towns. Violence and threats of violence thus denied suffragists the freedom of public political space in the South Wales towns.[24] A distinctly masculinist version of local and national identity was projected against the suffragist platform by the singing of the Welsh national anthem, 'Sosban Fach' and the 'New Zealand war chant', the last two linked with national pride and Welsh masculinity through the rugby field. The implication was that the suffragist cause lacked legitimacy in the face of national sentiment and male chauvinism (the anachronistic usage feels entirely apt), and that their presence in Cardiff was not to be suffered. In response, the women and their supporters attempted to deploy a different version of Welsh manliness: appealing to chivalry and respect, they called for 'a characteristic Welsh welcome'; when it wasn't forthcoming the demonstrators were asked to 'be men, have some respect for women; have some respect for courage'; Edward

Thomas (Cochfarf) shouted from the platform of the Cardiff's
Cory Hall that he was 'ashamed as a Welshman' – but he could be
heard no further back than the press table. In response the anti-
suffragists sang music-hall songs about gender confusion.[25]

These were partisan crowds; the Cardiff rioters hunted the
suffragists through the political geography of the town, from the
Cory Hall to the Unionist headquarters and then to the Ruskin
Institute, which was defended by 'stalwart socialists' while the
women held a small meeting. After a similar 'hooligan carnival' in
Aberdare in 1909, addressed by WSPU members Margaret
Mackworth (daughter of the local MP D. A. Thomas and the
suffragist Sybil Thomas) and Annie Kenney, Liberal men
expressed their satisfaction, in letters to the local newspaper, that
the suffragettes had got a taste of their own medicine. Liberal
women in the town, however, had supported the meeting, and
attempted to engage with the speakers: as suffragists, they wanted
the subject aired, and they wanted to distinguish between militant
and constitutional methods.[26] Those who broke up the meetings
were not interested in such distinctions.

The conditions under which women were now licensed to enter
the Liberal tent were demonstrated in April 1909, when the anti-
suffragist cabinet minister Lewis Harcourt addressed a ticketed
meeting of Cardiff Liberals.[27] Despite the fact that a number of
women were subscribers to the Liberal Association, women were
able to obtain tickets only through male members, who extracted a
pledge of good behaviour from them, and were then held
responsible for the behaviour of their guests. Women were excluded
from the body of the hall, confined to the balcony, distant from the
stage and – in the event of interjections – inaudible to most below.
As Harcourt ranged widely over government policy and issues of
the day, he provided ample openings to suffragettes to point out
the anomalous position of women, and there were three shouted
interjections. Only the first heckler was able to make her point; as
Harcourt spoke about taxation, she stood up in the balcony and
shouted, 'The tax is paid by women who want the vote' – an
impeccable Liberal suffragist position. After that, preventing the
words coming out of the women's mouths was as urgent as

ejecting them; the press described the second incident, as Harcourt spoke about tariffs versus free trade:

> At this point another suffragette made herself heard in the gallery. What she said was inaudible, but she was speedily silenced. A handkerchief was firmly held over her mouth, and she was passed towards the door, amid much good-natured chaff from the audience.[28]

It would be hard to find a more vivid image of the silencing of women.

In closing remarks both Harcourt and Guest made reference to the interjections. Harcourt said that 'he was glad to think there were many ladies in the balcony who did not hold his views, yet who had learned to respect the decencies of public meetings', while Guest expressed the belief that 'it would be found that those ladies who had not regard to the decencies of public meetings were not Cardiff people'. The right sort of women – local, and decently silent – were being contrasted to indecorous strangers. There was much emphasis in the reports on the good humour and light wit of the speakers and their audience in dealing with the hecklers, civilized masculine urbanity opposed to the indecency of the interruptions. As we have seen, the suggestion that women's protest was an importation, and therefore lacked legitimacy, had been made before in other ways. However, Harcourt's respect for local women who observed the 'decencies' did not extend to answering their written questions.[29]

The range of political issues covered by Harcourt allowed him to make frequent reference to 'the people': free trade and the 'cheap loaf', the 'Peers versus the people', the People's Budget; religious equality and Welsh desires for disestablishment; all gave plenty of scope for moving populist rhetoric. The irony was not lost on suffragists of all stripes in the audience. Ethel Lester Jones, daughter of the WLA president, whose father had a place on the platform, sent up a written question, asking 'how Mr Harcourt thought it possible for the Government to express the will of the people while the women had no votes'.[30] It was, of course, only the vocal interjections of the militants, and their suppression, which was reported by the press. The attempt at written questions was recorded in a letter, written in the heat of her anger immediately after the meeting by Dr Erie Evans, one of the founders of C&DWSS. Evans had obtained a ticket from Mr Lester Jones, having promised that she would be silent throughout, 'a pledge it was easy for me to give in as much as I am strongly opposed to any attempt to interfere with free speech'. Her protestations were a reference to the accusation that suffragettes, by interrupting meetings, showed themselves to be against free speech. In other circumstances, suffragists pointed out that free speech had traditionally meant the right of public assembly without interference from the authorities, not the silencing of individuals at meetings,[31] but Evans was demonstrating her reasonableness. She had been seated next to Ethel Lester Jones, who had consulted her about the question for Harcourt. That it was not answered was no surprise to the women, but Evans developed the bigger issue of women's place within the political nation, protesting at the way women's claims were increasingly cast outside the pale of legitimate political discourse:

> To quote the words of Mr. Bertram in the House of Commons on March 19th, members 'are not there as representing women, they were there as representing the men voters of the country'.[32]

Evans claimed that after the meeting, Mr Lester Jones had been censured by the CLA executive, amongst whom the feeling was that it was 'illegitimate for a woman to send up written questions at a public meeting'. Reasonable to a fault, Evans was willing to 'recognise that owing to our disfranchisement it is illegitimate for women to put *spoken* questions at public meetings, because they occupy time which might be used by a voter'[33] (or, she might have said, by a man, since no test of enfranchisement was applied to male questioners); but she expressed astonishment and dismay at the implications:

> . . . that it should be regarded as illegitimate for unenfranchised sections of the people to put *written* questions had never occurred to me . . . It is well for us to clearly understand what are the disabilities imposed on us by our disfranchisement . . .[34]

Women or the People? Political crises 1910–1911

The year 1910 was full of intersecting political events which had national and local significance for Liberal suffragists. Both general elections of 1910 were called in response to the constitutional crisis, and the government's determination to resolve it by the introduction of the Parliament Bill, which would limit the Lords' power of veto. When the January election produced a House of Commons without a strong majority, a cross-party approach to the question of women's suffrage was attempted, with the formation of a Conciliation Committee of MPs. The committee produced three Bills; the first had a successful second reading in July 1910, despite Cabinet opposition. However, when a general election was called for December it became clear that no further parliamentary time would be available.

The opposition to women's suffrage of the Prime Minister, Asquith, in the context of the complex politics of the years up to 1914, was crucial to the fate of the cause. However, it was Lloyd George who moved to the centre of suffragists' attention in 1910; having hitherto presented himself as a supporter of women's enfranchisement, he strenuously opposed the Conciliation Bill as being too narrow and undemocratic. For the militants, he henceforth stood for Liberal perfidy, and accounts and photographs of the violent treatment of suffragettes at his meetings, especially on his home ground in North Wales, have delivered him to posterity as an enemy of women's suffrage. The position was more fraught for Welsh Liberal suffragists: Lloyd George still held iconic status as a representative of Welsh national aspirations, acquired when as leader of Cymru Fydd he had appeared to embody the hopes of national progress, and reaching new heights as he attained greater national prominence.[35] Opposition to Lloyd George, or criticism of his position, might cast the suffragists beyond the pale of the nation, further de-legitimizing their claims, and drawing real hostility.

The Chancellor, in his turn, was wont to wrap himself in national sentiment and populist language, as in a flag, in response to challenges from suffragists. At the end of September, having made a strong attack on the 'undemocratic' character of the Bill in the House and outside it, he further annoyed suffragists nationally, but especially in Wales, when he told a delegation of local women at his home in Cricieth, that women's suffrage 'was not the cause which he had nearest his heart'. He was fighting, he said, 'the battle of the poor and oppressed'; he 'put first of all the causes I have at heart – Welsh Disestablishment, land reform, improvement of the condition of the masses . . . the cause of the people from whom I have sprung. I place them before anything else'.[36] When casting the House of Lords as the citadel of reactionary privilege, Lloyd George could speak eloquently and movingly of the evils of poverty.[37] 'The People' might then take on dual meaning: on one hand, all those united against power and privilege, which included Lloyd George and his audience; and at the same time, 'the poor and oppressed', the agents of whose deliverance the Liberals would be.[38] Here, however, 'the cause of the people' was further recast in terms of the causes of Cymru Fydd, and moreover connected to Lloyd George's own origins, which in Cymru Fydd mythology had made him an emblematic representative of Welshness.[39] 'The people' of Lloyd George's British discourse became the *gwerin* of the Welsh national story, as he addressed his Welsh constituency through his visitors. The four-woman delegation included active local Liberals, who protested at the Chancellor's assumption that they were not interested in the same causes as he. At this he declared that there was no better illustration of the defects of the Conciliation Bill than that women such as they, 'who had worked very hard for those causes would under this Bill have no voice at all in their settlement', thus, by rhetorical sleight, linking support for national causes and opposition to the Bill. The Chancellor had also explained to his visitors, as the newspaper headline put it, 'Why Wales is Unsympathetic', referring to militant incursions into 'their places of worship . . . their services . . . their national festival'. Distinctive national institutions – Wales itself, he seemed to suggest – were under attack, the suffragette actions were laid at the door of the whole women's movement, and Lloyd George's position became that of the nation.

A lengthy report of the meeting appeared in the *South Wales Daily News,* which was taking the Lloyd George line on the Bill.

In response, Olive Stevenson-Howell, secretary of the Cardiff WFL, protested at the Chancellor's intense identification with causes such as disestablishment, for which, she declared, there was now no demand.[40] She protested at the exclusiveness of that identification: 'a member, holding a responsible position, has no right to treat with comparative indifference reforms which do not happen to be nearest his particular heart.' She responded to his rhetoric of 'the poor and oppressed', and his claim that the Conciliation Bill was undemocratic, with a plea for the need of working women for representation: were not women, she asked, 'notoriously the worst paid class of workers and the most oppressed by sweating employers'; were women not 'to be included in the people?' Women would soon find their way to the Chancellor's heart, she suggested, if they withheld their taxes.[41] Responding to Lloyd George's rhetoric, Stevenson-Howell also divided the people, and women, into parts: since the first formulations of their demands for enfranchisement, women had based their claim on their status as taxpayers; but increasingly in the late nineteenth century, they had claimed citizenship for the sake of poor, oppressed and exploited women, both in Britain and in the Empire. Cardiff Liberal suffragists continued, in this period, to remind themselves that they wanted the vote 'to guard against tyrannical laws for women, both in England and India, especially in the interests of purity', to combat the 'white slave traffic', as well as to look after the interests of working women in Cardiff.[42] But Stevenson-Howell's letter signals the alienation of suffragists from the long-standing visions of Welsh nationhood. Her anger was vividly conveyed by her biting letter, as had been the anger of Erie Evans the previous year. In happier times, both would have been active Liberals; however, these were not women of the Cymru Fydd generation and, excluded from the Liberal conversation, they now declared that its terms were bogus.

The following day, it was announced that the Chancellor had given instructions that women were to be excluded from the annual meetings of the Welsh National Liberal Council (WNLC), to be held at Mountain Ash. WLAs had been affiliated to the WNLC since its formation in 1898, and while women's representation on the Council was weak, those women who kept up the connection included such party stalwarts as Maria Richards of Aberdare, Susannah Gee from Denbigh, Kate Freeman of Swansea, and Lady Brynmor Jones, all of whom, in the 1890s, had been instrumental in building women's Liberal organisation, and in bringing male and female Liberalism closer. 'A number of resignations' from women followed, and the Hospitality Committee rather timidly asked Lloyd George that women who were hostesses for the meetings should be allowed to attend. In the event, the meetings were cancelled when a general election was announced,[43] but the damage done was not cancelled. The Council's Conventions represented 'the idea of the political unity – almost the general will – of a nation',[44] a nation from which women could be excluded, it seemed, by edict.

Losing Cardiff

The national crisis, and the deteriorating relations between the Government and the women's movement, came together in Cardiff in the last three months of 1910. The suffragist MP D. A. Thomas was about to retire. With the lesson learned from their support for Ivor Guest in 1906, the prominent part taken by other Welsh Liberal MPs against Suffrage Bills over the last two or three years, and with Lloyd George's hostility providing legitimacy to Welsh anti-suffragists, the Cardiff WLA executive called a national conference of Welsh Liberal women. The conference was an attempt to produce a united voice in support of the Conciliation Bill, but it was also intended to go further, with an application of the 'test question' in Wales: that WLAs should refuse electoral help to candidates whose position on women's suffrage was not satisfactory. The conference was reported at great length by the Cardiff press, under headlines like 'Welshwomen in fighting mood. Boycott of Liberal MPs', and 'Vote Before Party. Liberal Women's Resolve'. The meeting was haunted by the absent Lloyd George, as one speaker after another referred to him, beginning with the president in her opening remarks: she continued, she said, to believe that he was a supporter of women's suffrage. The resolution, asking that the period of truce in Parliament be used to pass the Bill into law, was moved by Mary Lloyd of Aberdare, an impeccable representative of old Nonconformist Liberalism. The preamble, 'that this conference while reaffirming its demands for Welsh Disestablishment . . . ', was a pointed reference to Lloyd George's argument with Welsh suffragists, and a sign that as yet Liberal suffragists, unlike the non-party campaigners like Stevenson-Howell, felt the need to placate the old radical sentiments of Wales. The resolution was carried unanimously. There were only three dissentients to the potentially more divisive resolution put by Kate Jones,[45] which proposed that, should the government not grant facilities for the bill, Liberal women should cease work for their party until the vote was won, and that in the coming election, they should work only for Liberals who supported the Conciliation Bill. The resolution was 'a challenge to all Liberal women to do something practical in their own cause' and to 'bring some pressure on [the Chancellor] as the Welsh Liberal leader'.[46] However, Lloyd George increased his majority in the December election. The meeting, despite appearances, was not indicative of strength or unity in women's Liberal organisation in Wales. The main impact was to be felt in Cardiff.

When the Cardiff Liberal Association announced that it had invited Sir Clarendon Hyde, an anti-suffragist businessman, to be their candidate,[47] the executive of the WLA quickly announced that in line with the conference resolution, the association would not work for Hyde's election. A split in the association immediately emerged, to be cynically exploited by Hyde and his agents. A number of women active in the WLA held a meeting with Lady Clarendon Hyde, giving rise to a report that 'the women Liberals of Cardiff are enthusiastic in the people's fight against the Peers, and . . . determined to do their part in securing victory'. Hyde issued the report as an election leaflet, with the message 'Men of Cardiff – The Women want you to Vote thus: Hyde X'.[48] Suffragists must have ground their teeth at this exploitation of unenfranchised women by a candidate who would deny them the vote. Numbers of the anti-Hyde camp took themselves off to other constituencies, notably Swansea, to work for suffragist candidates. The constitutional crisis was too serious for them to remain idle during the election – women Liberals had a long history of opposition to the power of the unelected peers – but the bitter experience of Cardiff politics in recent years had made them determined to work only for 'the right candidate',[49] Cardiff was lost to Ninian Crichton Stuart, who had given the right answers on women's suffrage to the C&DWSS. According to his wife – and it must have given satisfaction to report it – 'a great number of women workers of all classes' had helped in his election.

In the post-mortems on 'Who Lost Cardiff?' women who had withdrawn their support from Hyde got their share of the blame, which they were happy to accept, since it demonstrated the importance of the women's associations in election work. Blaming the women went further: despite their protestations that 'there were no truer Liberals', they were also accused of 'treachery', indicative of the extent to which it was assumed that women would and should set aside their own political aims at such a time, while the various categories of male voters who had stayed away from the poll or given their vote elsewhere were regarded as having legitimate political reservations. It was 'treachery' because women's efforts were deemed to belong to the party, or to the 'cause' of Liberalism, and never to themselves; the language of altruistic Liberalism, of duty and citizenship, which women themselves had done so much to develop, was turned against them.[50] There might be 'no truer Liberals', but they were, over the next few months, to redefine their Liberalism. They retained, they declared, their belief that 'the full representation of the people' was a 'Liberal principle', but they had their self-respect to consider.[51] Now there was no attempt to conciliate the old Welsh party: WLA president Edith Lester Jones declared 'that woman suffrage was of more importance even than Home Rule and Disestablishment'. The declaration indicated the distance travelled: home rule and disestablishment, with the enfranchisement of women and support for temperance, had formed the four fixed points of political identity for Welsh women Liberals in the 1890s. After being censured by the party, Lester Jones, four of her vice-presidents, eight members of the executive committee, and many ordinary members, resigned from the WLA to form the Cardiff Progressive Liberal Women's Union in April 1911. There came a time, said Lester Jones, 'when they had to put principle before anything else . . . when they saw some of the best of their women leaving them, it was time for them to consider their position'.[52]

As the formation of the new society shows, these women had not cut themselves off from Liberalism, but they had fundamentally redefined what their Liberalism meant, rejecting the language of Welsh Radicalism: the term 'Progressive' in WLF circles had long signified those who put their own enfranchisement first, and this is what many women in South Wales now decided to do. Women's Liberal organisation in South Wales went into decline, and in Cardiff the rump WLA disappeared into the Ladies' Social Committee of the Liberal Association, while the Progressives remained a small and ineffectual group into the post-war years.[53] It might be argued that there had long been at least two WLAs in Cardiff, one looking towards the party, interested in support and fundraising, doing what Aberdare WLA had memorably described as 'quiet work for the Liberal Party'; the other having a clear political agenda of its own, to which women's enfranchisement was central, and seen as in conformity with the frequently invoked 'Liberal principles'. Both would have seen themselves as ardent, loyal and 'true' Liberals. These differences could in the normal run of things be accommodated within the structures of a large association, where there was plenty of work of different kinds for all to do. But the conditions of 1910-11 were not in the normal run of things: into the mixture of constitutional and political crisis was thrown the insulting indifference of the party to the political desires of the women they relied on for electoral work. What had appeared to be a large and strong WLA then split along a natural fault, in a way which appears to have destroyed it as a political force. However, as Cardiff WLA collapsed, the C&DWSS waxed mighty, reaching a membership of over one thousand – as the WLA had once done. It can reasonably be said that the suffrage societies replaced women's Liberal organisation in Cardiff and South Wales.[54]

Conclusion

In the late nineteenth century, women had been able to identify
with, and expand, the language of altruistic Liberalism, producing
a highly developed discourse of citizenship as 'womanly duty'.[55]
In Wales, the closeness of this to the agenda of Welsh
Nonconformity had meant that the progress of women and of the
nation was seen as advancing 'hand in hand'. It has been argued
that English feminism abandoned the language of populism,
replacing it with 'womanhood' in the 1880s and 1890s.[56] The
national resurgence of the Cymru Fydd period, during which
women placed themselves at 'the spoken centre'[57] of the Welsh
national conversation, enabled 'womanhood' and 'the people' to
retain their connection rather longer in the Welsh context. That
connection weakened after 1895 under the impact of divisions in
Wales. In the crisis of Liberalism of the Edwardian years, a
popular masculinist nationalism was deployed by the Liberal
crowd, while the party's refusal to take women's political
ambitions seriously combined with its deployment of the old
'idiom of dissent' to enforce party loyalty, and to delegitimize the
voice of unenfranchised women. It was at one level a battle for
possession of political spaces, the right to a presence, to speak
certain words and be heard to speak them. That battle was easily
won, in the short term, by aggressive masculinity. At another level,
words were themselves the area of contestation; it was about the
relationship of women to the Liberal Party, and it was about their
relationship to the language of radical liberalism. However, the
context should not be forgotten. It was not inevitable that national
feeling should be roused against 'incomers' and 'alien' ideas. The
robust patriarchalism of Welsh society is not an adequate
explanation.[58] Nor, alternatively, the threatened masculinity of the
public sphere. All of these might have been conjured up in the
1890s, when national feeling was at its height, but when, in
contrast, there was enthusiastic support for women's role in public
life and their enfranchisement, and a warm welcome for visiting
women speakers who came to spread the message. By 1908,
transgressive militancy had licensed men to abandon chivalry
towards middle-class ladies, but in a very specific context: as the

Liberal government moved into the constitutional crisis of its sought-for confrontation with the Lords, the challenge from women who had once been relied on as the party's 'natural' supporters was not to be endured. By spring of 1911, while the damage to Liberalism endured, the context had changed; Liberal and Labour suffragists, local women and visitors together, occupied the stage of the Cory Hall with a large and appreciative audience, even as, in the House of Commons, Lloyd George voted in favour of the second Conciliation Bill.[59]

NOTES

[1] Manifesto of Cardiff Liberal suffragists; *South Wales Daily News* (*SWDN*), 10 March 1911. My thanks to Angela John and Neil Evans, who generously read and commented on an early draft of this chapter. They will see that I have taken up some, but not all of their very interesting suggestions, mainly for reasons of time and space. Similarly, thanks to the editor of this collection, T. Robin Chapman.

[2] Helen Fraser, NUWSS organiser, speaking at Bridgend; *Glamorgan Gazette* 10 November 1911.

[3] There is an increasingly rich literature on the topic. See, for example: Jane Rendall, 'Citizenship, Culture and Civilisation: the language of British suffragists 1866–1874', in Caroline Daley and Melanie Nolan (eds.), *Suffrage and Beyond: International Feminist Perspectives* (New York, 1994); Helen Rogers, *Women and the People: Authority, Authorship and the Radical Tradition in Nineteenth Century England* (Aldershot, 2000; Jon Lawrence, 'Contesting the Male Polity: The Suffragettes and the Politics of Disruption in Edwardian Britain', in Amanda Vickery (ed.), *Women, Privilege, and Power: British Politics 1750 to the Present* (Stanford, California 2001); Laura E. Nym Mayhall, 'The Rhetorics of Slavery and Citizenship: suffragist discourse and canonical texts in Britain, 1880–1914', *Gender & History*, Vol. 13, November 2001, 481–97.

[4] U. Masson, '"Hand in hand with the women, forward we will go": Welsh nationalism and feminism in the 1890s', *Women's History Review*, 12 (2003), 357–86.

[5] Angela V. John, '"Run like blazes": the suffragettes and Welshness', *Llafur: Journal of Welsh Labour History*, 6, 3, (1994), 28–43; *idem*, '"A Draft of Fresh Air"'. Women's Suffrage, the Welsh and London', *Transactions of the Honourable Society of Cymmrodorion*, 1994–5, 81–93; *idem*, '"Chwarae Teg": Welsh Men's Support for Women's Suffrage', Welsh Political Archive Lecture 1997, (Aberystwyth, 1998). For more on the theme, Kay Cook & Neil Evans, '"The Petty Antics of the Bell-Ringing, Boisterous Band"? The Women's Suffrage Movement in Wales, 1890–1918', in Angela V. John (ed.) *Our Mothers' Land: Chapters in Welsh Women's History 1830-1939* (Cardiff, 1991), 180–1; Ceridwen Lloyd-Morgan, 'From Temperance to Suffrage', in *ibid.*, 154.

[6] John, 'Run Like Blazes', 32; Cook & Evans, 'The Petty Antics', 180–1.

[7] John, 'Chwarae Teg', 5–6.

[8] Claire Hirshfield, 'Fractured faith: Liberal Party women and the suffrage issue in Britain, 1892–1914', *Gender and History* 2 (1990), 180–93; Martin Pugh, 'The Limits of Liberalism: Liberals and women's suffrage, 1867–1914', in Eugenio F. Biagini (ed.), *Citizenship and Community: Liberals, Radicals and Collective Identities in the British Isles, 1865–1931* (Cambridge, 1996), 64–5.

[9] The Women's Liberal Federation (WLF) was the England and Wales body to which local WLAs were affiliated.

[10] This summary is based on research in a range of sources including local newspapers, the records of the Cardiff WLA, the Welsh Union of Women's Liberal Associations (WUWLA) and the Women's Liberal Federation (WLF), and Cardiff City Council. See also Ryland Wallace, *Organise! Organise! Organise!: A Study of Reform Agitations in Wales, 1840–1886* (Cardiff, 1991), Chapter XI.

[11] In the extended Guest family, however, there were also a number of active suffragists; I am grateful to Angela John for this information.

[12] *Hansard,* HoC Deb. March 16 1904, division list 58; HoC Deb. Feb. 28 1908, c. 279, division list 28; WLF *Summary* IV/6 Dec. 10 1905, IV/8 Feb. 10 1906; *SWDN,* 3 March, 5 June 1908, 18–19 March 1909; Brian Harrison, *Separate Spheres: the Opposition to Women's Suffrage in Britain* (London 1978) 122, 127. There were few branches of the anti-suffrage organisations in Wales until 1913, when seventeen branches appeared; Cardiff had an active branch in 1910–11.

[13] *SWDN,* 15 June, 4 July 1908.

[14] Jon Lawrence, *Speaking for the People: Party, Language and Popular Politics in England, 1867–1914* (Cambridge, 1998) Ch. 7, esp. 190–1; *idem,* 'Contesting the Male Polity', 201–226. I am much indebted to Lawrence's work, and to Helen Rogers, *Women and the People,* in thinking about these events in Wales.

[15] Martin Pugh, *The March of the Women: a Revisionist Analysis of the campaign for Women's Suffrage, 1866–1914* (Oxford, 2000) 188–91.

[16] *SWDN,* May–June 1908.

[17] The NUWSS was the largest suffrage society, formed as an umbrella organisation in 1897, and in this period building and restructuring, partly in response to militancy; it was strictly constitutional in tactics. The WFL was a 'soft militant' organisation, a breakaway from the WSPU.

[18] *SWDN,* 12 May 1908.

[19] The WFL policy was not to interrupt speakers but 'to ask questions at the time allowed;' *The Times* 23 January 1908.

[20] Pugh, *March of the Women,* 136–7.

[21] Hirshfield, 'Fractured Faith', 181.

[22] Jon Lawrence, 'Contesting the Male Polity', 201–226.

[23] *SWDN,* 14 May 1908.

[24] *SWDN,* 12 May 1908; Lawrence, *Representing the People,* 190–191; *idem,* 'Contesting the Male Polity', 201–4.

[25] *SWDN,* 12–14 May 1908, 25 May 1908.

[26] U. Masson (ed.), *Women's Rights and 'Womanly Duties': the Aberdare Women's Liberal Association 1891–1910* (Cardiff, 2005) 72–3; *SWDN,* 12 May 1908. For more on Liberal disruption of suffrage meetings at about this time, in the Rhondda, see Elizabeth Andrews, *A Woman's Work is Never Done* (Ystrad Rhondda, 1956) and reprinted in *A Woman's Work is Never Done: autobiographies and political writing, 1923–48* [ed. Ursula Masson] forthcoming from Honno: Welsh Women's Press, 2006).

[27] Cochfarf collection, Box 7, letter from Erie Evans 2 May 1909; *SWDN,* 3 April 1909.

[28] *SWDN,* 3 April 1909.

[29] Erie Evans, *loc. cit.*

[30] By 1912, the whole Lester family was enrolled in C&DWSS.

[31] *The Times,* 8 October 1908, Emmeline Pethick-Lawrence, in an exchange of letters with Lloyd George.

[32] Erie Evans, 2 April 1909.

[33] *Ibid.,* emphasis original. 19 March 1909 was the date of the second reading debate on Howard's Adult Suffrage Bill.

[34] Evans, *loc cit.,* emphasis original.

[35] Neil Evans, '"A Nation in a Nutshell": the Swansea disestablishment demonstration of 1912 and the political culture of Edwardian Wales', 218–9. in

R. R. Davies and Geraint H. Jenkins (eds.), *From Medieval to Modern Wales: Historical Essays in Honour of Kenneth O. Morgan and Ralph A. Griffiths* (Cardiff, 2004), 218–9.

[36] *SWDN*, 29 September 1910.

[37] *The Times*, 2 October 1908.

[38] On the division of the body of 'the People' into 'different parts with varying capacities' in radical discourse, Rogers, *Women and the People*, 7.

[39] Ursula Masson, 'Gender and National Memory: *Young Wales*, 1895–1903', unpublished paper presented to the Fourth Conference of the North American association for the Study of Welsh Culture and History, Le Moyne College, New York, June 2002.

[40] Some commentators at the time observed, and the judgement of historians since has been, that the disestablishment issue '[i]ncreasingly . . . was beginning to lose its primacy in Welsh life', particularly in South Wales and that Lloyd George had himself lost interest in the question, though he was obliged to support it; Kenneth O. Morgan, *Wales in British Politics 1866–1922* (Cardiff, 1980), 240, 273–4; Evans, 'A Nation in a Nutshell'.

[41] The Tax Resistance League, formed in October 1909, included on its 1910 committee Kate Freeman, a leading figure in Welsh women's Liberal politics, and a member of the Welsh National Liberal Council (WLNC); Crawford, *The Women's Suffrage Movement*, 671–2.

[42] *SWDN*, 24 March 1908, 1 October 1910.

[43] *SWDN*, September–October 1910.

[44] Evans, 'A Nation in a Nutshell', 216–7.

[45] Usually known as Mrs Viriamu Jones, a long-time Liberal, suffragist and temperance activist, wife of the principal of the University College.

[46] *SWDN, WM*, 4 November 1910.

[47] *SWDN*, 14–16 November 1910. Hyde had been MP for Wednesbury 1900–1910.

[48] *SWDN*, 25-26 November 1910; election leaflet, NLW Welsh Political Ephemera Box XJN 1165.

[49] *WM, SWDN*, November–December 1910.

[50] Jane Rendall, 'Citizenship', 127–50.

[51] *SWDN*, 10 March 1911.

[52] *WM, SWDN*, December 1910–March 1911.

[53] *SWDN*, 11–15 March 1912.

[54] U. Masson, 'Divided loyalties: women's suffrage and party politics in South Wales 1912–1915', *Llafur: Journal of Welsh Labour History*, 7, 3 & 4, (1998/9), 119–20.

[55] Jane Rendall, 'Citizenship', 127–50; Mayhall, 'The Rhetorics' on what this language owed to the influence on feminists of Mazzini.

[56] Rogers, *Women and the People*, 283–301.

[57] The phrase is Patrick Joyce's: he suggests that Gladstonian discourses brought women to 'the spoken centre' of Liberalism in the 1880s, though without endowing them with any power; Joyce, 'The constitution and the narrative structure of Victorian politics', in James Vernon (ed.), *Re-reading the constitution: New narratives in the political history of England's long nineteenth century* (Cambridge, 1996), 196–7. I have suggested elsewhere (Masson, 'Hand in hand'), that in the Welsh context of the early 1890s, women were active agents

in shaping political discourses, but that this did not give them a secure hold on influence in Welsh Liberalism.

[58] Kenneth O. Morgan, *Rebirth of a Nation: Wales 1880–1980* (Oxford & Cardiff, 1982), 137.

[59] *SWDN*, 6 May 1911.

THEISM'S LAST HURRAH: SAUNDERS LEWIS'S CAERNARFON COURT SPEECH OF 1936

T. Robin Chapman

Saunders Lewis didn't let the facts get in the way of a good title. The booklet that the Bangor students sold for 3d each on the streets outside the assizes in Caernarfon on 13 October 1936, *Why We Burnt the Bombing School*,[1] was not the story of the arson of an RAF training establishment; all that he and his co-accused, the Fishguard schoolmaster D. J. Williams and the Llandudno-based Baptist minister Lewis Valentine had done five weeks before, on 8 September, was to set light to a few workmen's huts and a pile of timber in the north-western corner of a building site in the Llŷn Peninsula. The affected area was roughly the same size as a cricket square, the property was not that of the Crown, as the prosecution argued, but the Glasgow contractors, and a decent defence counsel could probably have won the case on a technicality. Indeed, the option was considered and rejected. 'My recollection', Lewis wrote to D. J. Williams's barrister on the fortieth anniversary of the trial, 'is that we were afraid you might get us off, which would have been very awkward.'[2] Moreover, the name by which this cause célèbre of nationalist civil disobedience subsequently became known, Penyberth, was similarly a misnomer. The house that had stood on the site, complete with its watchtower to warn of invaders, had been levelled a week before the attack. The hearing ended in glorious confusion when the jury failed to agree on a verdict, and Lewis and Williams were carried shoulder-high through the streets. Valentine, for the record, was too heavy to receive the same acclaim.

Dafydd Glyn Jones wrote in the early 1970s that 'Wales is still trying to assimilate the meaning of the fire at Penyberth, and will continue to do so for many years to come.'[3] At a roughly equal distance from the comment to that which the commentator himself was from the event, one can at least attempt to understand why and how it mattered – and matters. As a practical protest, like the Yoko Ono installation at London's Indica Gallery, where she first met John Lennon, Penyberth was an imaginary nail hammered into an imaginary block of wood for the payment of an imaginary five shillings. Even in an obituary to Lewis, one supporter called it 'a complete failure' as a tactic.[4] The training facility opened in May 1938, and only a dangerously inhospitable climate and a remote location eventually forced it to close.

One can assess the political effects of the action, too. Although the precise figures are sketchy (even prominent supporters were negligent when it came to paying their fees), Nationalist Party membership rose by a few hundred, and the number of branches increased from 72 to 94 between August 1936 and August 1937; but the enthusiasm did not translate itself into electoral success. The party organizer, J. E. Jones, making the best of a bad job, spoke of the late 1930s as a period of 'consistent strong slow progress'.[5] For successive Plaid Cymru leaders, and Gwynfor Evans more than any, Penyberth certainly mattered: the story of his presidency was a nimble sidling away from its discourse of sacrifice. When he captured the party's first seat, at a by-election in Carmarthen thirty years later, he did so despite Penyberth rather than because of it.

Its personal significance for Lewis was real enough. As two generations of Welsh nationalists could repeat like a mantra, a re-trial was held at the Old Bailey in January 1937, the three were found guilty and jailed for nine months at Wormwood Scrubs, and he was dismissed from his lectureship. A. J. P. Taylor remarked waspishly when Lewis's address was published alongside pieces by Hazlitt, Sydney Smith, Thomas Carlyle, William Morris and Robert Louis Stephenson, that it was an unconsciously ironic text. Its defence of Welsh decency contrasted sharply with the indecency of the action taken against him by his compatriots: 'If Mr Saunders Lewis achieved the independent Wales of his dreams, he would undoubtedly be flung into prison, if not burnt alive. As it is, his martyrdom (thanks to English protection) has been gentle in the extreme; after all no one can regard the position of a lecturer at Swansea University College as something of which one is deprived with regret'.[6] Lewis would make a precarious living as a freelance journalist, teacher and schools inspector for the next fifteen years.

Penyberth also mattered as a story that nationalists told themselves: a narrative with heroes and villains, obduracy and honour and, in the public meetings that punctuated its progress, a cast of thousands. In the late 1970s and early 1980s, when Radio Cymru saw it as its mission to preserve race memory, elderly men and women would tell how they had seen the flames light the sky on that windy September morning; how they attended the May 1936 rally on the square in Pwllheli, where Saunders Lewis had stood on a children's roundabout to address a crowd of 7,000, holding the microphone high as he spoke to avoid the grasping hands of local youths determined to prevent him. Others were among the two hundred or so who travelled to London on a chartered train in January 1937, singing hymns for the Fleet Street press outside the Old Bailey at five o'clock in the morning; and a privileged few recalled how they had squeezed into the gallery of Number One Court to watch the action. Still others were among the 5,000 who crammed the Guildhall in Swansea in May 1937 to hear a dozen speakers – including Labour councillors and former students – call for his reinstatement, or the 12,000 who witnessed the triumphal return of the three to the Pavilion in Caernarfon in September of the same year, in what was described as the biggest indoor gathering in Welsh history, with some of the more adventurous perching in the rafters to gain a better view and hear Saunders Lewis compare the fire to the Boston Tea Party as an act of anti-colonial defiance.

When Dafydd Glyn Jones pondered Penyberth's 'meaning' in the early 1970s, he was using the word as shorthand for its political and cultural implications after the event. This paper approaches the same word from the opposite direction. It looks at the event's 'meaning' for Lewis on that October afternoon, without the benefit of hindsight. In this second sense, his address to the jury in Caernarfon, two days before his forty-third birthday, was a culmination rather than a beginning, an attempt to wrest Penyberth from his own party and his co-accused, from those who had attended the meetings and signed the petitions, from the jury and the remembrancers, from history itself. For him, the significance of Penyberth was that, for the first time, he had applied the discourse of his art and spirituality to the arena of political protest. He described it to an interviewer as 'a symbolic act, an act for Wales, an act to prove to the English government that not all the leaders of Wales were cowards who could be mocked'.[7] His speech, too, like the arson that had prompted it, was a sacramental act: theism's last hurrah in nationalist protest.

For Lewis, the discourse of signification – image, symbol, sign, type, icon – was an accretion of critical devices that over time amounted to a metaphysics. He first employed it to express his distaste for naturalistic theatre. In a series of newspaper articles in 1920, he argued that 'the aim of a scene in a play is to make suggestions to the spirit, not to satisfy the lusts of the eye',[8] called Ibsen 'the most inartistic and harmful influence that ever ascended to the throne of art',[9] and suggested that his 'bare, brash realism' could be tempered by the use of costume that reflected the mood of the characters: 'cold colours, green or grey on a dark background' to convey dejection and 'warm colours, red and orange' to show joy.[10] When symbols are used to explain human emotion, he wrote of Caradog Prichard's *pryddest*, 'Y Briodas' ('The Wedding', 1927), where Mountain, River, Yew and Spirit act as contradictory choruses, the poet operates *sub specie aeternitatis*:

There are at least two types of writer. For one, what is important is men and their thoughts and tricks and interaction one with another. This writer sees human life as a brief period of light between two blacknesses: the infinity that precedes it and the infinity that comes after . . .

There is another type of writer . . . Unlike the other he cannot close off the cosy room of human enjoyment from the night that surrounds him. The darkness is an urgent pressure on him, it calls on him, closes on him, so that the light of human life is only a guttering candle in his hand. He cannot ignore the darkness, because it is full of voices and pictures that are as close to him as brothers. He can only accept them as part of his life and be content with the dreadful loneliness that is his fate.[11]

Lewis brought a complementary attitude to his criticism of the Welsh literary tradition. His 1925 essay on the fifteenth-century strict-metre poet Dafydd Nanmor uses the work to explain what Lewis calls 'the Welsh Aesthetic'. Again, the criticism turns on signs and signifiers. Dafydd Nanmor, Lewis argues, functions as a channel. He is the poet of the noble house. His poems about fine silks and the women who wear them, food and wine, furniture, decoration and good company are composed in praise of 'the sensual and sacramental elements in life'. They exhibit palpable pleasure in palpable things, but use these, too, as symbols. These material delights are symbols of *perchentyaeth*: the belief that owning such a house, and the noble lineage this implies, brings with it duties of patronage, hospitality and the maintenance of culture. According to Lewis's interpretation of the 'Welsh Aesthetic', the luxuries that Dafydd describes have their signifiers in continuity and survival, and this is as true of Dafydd's poems as of their subject matter: 'Some works of art', Lewis concludes, 'are a symbol of a complete civilization, and they endure, after the age that has produced them has disappeared, as a picture of the best of that age's learning and desire'.[12]

He took 'the Welsh Aesthetic' as the title of the opening chapter of his *Williams Pantycelyn*, published two years later. Medieval praise poetry, he asserts, is 'a sign of faith in civilization and a sign of faith in life'. It presupposes 'that there is order in creation, that Existence is an infallible system, and that there is a harmony that can be heard underneath all the clamour of facts'. Music and poetry for the medieval mind were 'symbols of the harmony of creation',[13] and the function of the praise the poets sang was 'to turn the senses into a medium for possessing perfection'.[14]

In the year between 'Dafydd Nanmor' and *Pantycelyn*, Lewis offered a taxonomy of symbol. Written ostensibly as a criticism of the excesses of the Gorsedd of Bards, his 'Pageantry or Sacrament'[15] is a more general assault on a Nonconformist Liberalism – 'the state of the Welsh mind in our age' – for embracing show (he cites Nonconformist ministers' fondness for wearing gowns in the pulpit) but rejecting the sacramentalism that gives it meaning. The sacrament of the Mass, he tells his readers, is not a reminder of Christ's sacrifice; it is the act re-enacted.

'Without that there is no mass. Without the display and the pageantry, nothing essential is lost. But without the sacrament, there is no reason for anything or any cause or excuse for any ritual at all [. . .] An unsymbolic symbol is as bad as salt that has no savour.' When he berates Wales for losing 'its faith in sacramentalism and sacramental religion', he disparages it as much for its tastelessness as for theological error. The loss of a sacramental mentality has made Wales 'superficial, materialistic and idolatrous', and its cultural history since the eighteenth century has been a continuous, vain attempt to replace it.

His *Braslun o Hanes Llenyddiaeth Gymraeg* (*Sketch of Welsh Literature*, 1932) shows the magnitude of that loss. In it Lewis traces the symbolism that sustains the medieval mind back to Taliesin in the sixth century and forward to the Act of Union one thousand years later, in an epic Platonic, Aristotelian and Thomist choreography of word and image. He states that by the twelfth and thirteenth centuries, in the work of the *Gogynfeirdd*, or Poets of the Princes, Taliesin's symbols of noble virtue, his eagle, lion, tower and anchor, in apposition or fashioned into new compounds with adjectives, are sufficient in themselves to convey meaning. There is no need for the impedimenta of prepositions, conjunctions, articles. The later practitioners of bardic tradition can dispense with the realism of syntax, like the players in their coloured costumes can dispense with the drawing-room stage. As the Middle Ages progress, words have developed an 'aura' that distinguishes their literal meaning (what Lewis calls their 'bare meaning') from their aesthetic function:

> A word's *aura* is its complex appeal to the senses and the feelings. The Welsh word 'rhin' [mystery, enchantment] almost serves as a translation. A word can be sweet-sounding to the ear; it can look pretty on paper; those are the elements of its *rhin*. But the *aura* comes especially from a word's associations, from the memory we have of hearing it before in important circumstances. Therefore, when a word is picked up afresh it brings with it the savour and imprints of deeply remembered experiences.[16]

As the tradition progresses, the bardic grammars of the fourteenth century systematize these same symbols within a hierarchy. Poetry becomes 'not only a symbol of ideal government, but a picture of a perfect unified society, the whole of creation and the entire system of being'.[17] The innumerable poems in praise of noble patrons are implicitly written in praise of God, and become 'a picture of Welsh Christian civilization, spread across a myriad bright hearths'.[18] By the fifteenth and early sixteenth centuries, there is a shift from the general to the particular, from Christian Platonism to Christian Aristotelianism, but the 'unity', as Lewis puts it, remains. Each nobleman, whatever his individual traits, is part of the whole, the nation is the sum of its families and art is a craft practised in praise of the creator.

His own creative work grew as what he would later call 'a logical enlargement of the Taliesinic tradition . . . the doctrine of correspondence'.[19] He published just two poems before Penyberth, and both hinge on perception through symbol. It is worth quoting the first, 'Llygad y Dydd yn Ebrill' ('A Daisy in April', 1928), albeit in translation, in full:

Yesterday I saw a daisy,
like a mirror of daybreak's beauty;
the day before, I trod heedless,
and yesterday, saw. How well I know
spring's passionate vigour and zest
creating its crystal shilling,
the force of the moorland's art,
ruby and gem in the marsh.
The field where the April cuckoo
sang has turned Milky Way;
the firmament's topsy-turvy,
millions of heaven's suns
are underfoot, put in place
to gild earth's pallid lawn;
Orion on the hill-breasts,
Arcturus and Sirius there,
butterflies' beads of fire,
like stars awake, seraphic,
on a blue resplendent sky.
Yesterday I saw a daisy.[20]

Despite appearances, the poem is determinedly non-lyrical. A lyric poet may have praised the daisy for its own simple beauty, or taken it as an occasion to write about childhood or his beloved, or as a parable of reincarnation or innocence. Lewis does none of these: 'Llygad y Dydd' is a manifesto for signification. His symbols do not represent; they connect. The word that carries the weight of all that follows is 'saw'. The day before yesterday he saw the daisy merely as a daisy and passed it by; yesterday he knew it by its resonances. He sees it as a shilling, a gem in the marsh, and then – as the panorama extends – the Milky Way, suns in the heavens, the constellations of Orion, Arcturus and Sirius, living coals. To experience the world through the senses alone, the poem implies, is not to see it as it really is. The daisy's significance doesn't lie in its own beauty, nor its ability to evoke any experience in the poet himself; it lies, rather, in its potential to alert the poet to its correspondences. Lewis chooses his figures of speech advisedly. The only simile in the poem comes in the second line: the daisy is 'like' a mirror of the heavens. All the images that follow are introduced by predicatives. The daisies *are* stars and suns in the same way that a face in a mirror remains a face.

The same dual perception occurs in 'I'r Sagrafen Fendigaid' ('To the Blessed Sacrament', 1936, published on the eve of the Caernarfon trial). Here, however, the perspective is turned on its head. Lewis's 'anti-papist friends', as he calls them, visiting a Catholic church, cannot see what the poet sees. He asks God, the paragon of *perchentyaeth*, not to be 'vexed' by his visitors' apparent discourtesy. For them, he says

> [. . .] your hall is nothing
> But an altar, its flowers and candlesticks helter-skelter and jumbled
> Like a full sideboard in a second-hand furniture shop.
> And sorry laughable pictures of your Passion and your Cross,
> And images in Brummagem plaster of Joseph and Mary
> Standing like an Aunt Sally at the fair,
> And Saint Theresa like a fashion plate in *Vogue* . . .
>
> Since who in his right mind,
> Lacking a better candle,
> (Oh Father of lights),

Would ever perceive you playing hide-and-seek with your land
In the form of wheat,
An insignificant scrap in all of the clutter?
No wonder the children will not kneel to their missing Lord.[21]

The visitors' blindness to the *Mysterium Tremendum* in the
overstuffed church, making unsymbolic symbols of the statues and
holy pictures, is not hostility but the collective forgetfulness of a
Christianity that has lost its ability to interpret what it sees through
the lens of faith. 'Wales', Lewis told an audience of Catholics a
year after his conversion, in 1934, 'has never accepted a
completely secular view of the world. She has never sought to
produce purely secular literature [. . .] But Welsh life and literature
have been plundered of the Sacraments of Catholic Christianity
from the fifteenth century until today.' As a result, Lewis argues,
'Welsh literature remains morbidly and gloriously attached to an
anti-secular and anti-humanistic philosophy, and it is morbid
because it does not possess the sacramentalism that would free it
and enable it to enjoy material creation.'

The Dafydd Nanmor essay was published in the same year that
Lewis co-founded the Welsh Nationalist Party, becoming its
president and editor of its monthly, *Y Ddraig Goch*, a year later.
The idiom of his early political writing, too, underscores the
signification in his critical and creative output, and his
pronouncements on the state of Wales, like his daisies, open
themselves like a mirror to heaven. In his first contribution,
arguably the nearest thing he ever wrote to a manifesto, running to
approximately 2,500 words and setting out 'all our doctrine and all
our hopes',[22] he uses the name 'Wales' only four times, and then
only to anticipate his readers' surprise that he does not intend to
discuss party policy with regard to the language, education and
industry. He begins, rather, by defining humanity under God: 'We
are Christians in a Christian country . . . and a Christian cannot
think politically without believing that it is right for men to live
joyfully and with dignity and to fulfil the potential of their nature'.
The nation is the medium for that fulfilment, 'the normal form of
society in Europe' and 'the basic principle' of the Nationalist Party
is 'to look at man as the product of the nation, and seek his welfare

as part of it, its son, its heir, a gentleman'.[23] In the same way that the House and its luxuries in Dafydd Nanmor's *cywyddau* are symbols of cultural continuity and survival, the nation here is the symbol of human joy and dignity under God. Man is not fully understood as man outside it. A nation, moreover, depends on its inhabitants' access to capital. It is 'a symbol of his freedom and his indebtedness'.[24]

Enough has been said about Lewis as critic, creative writer and politician for the reader to infer a fourth element: his personal flamboyance. A student, and later a friend, remarked that Lewis's entire professional life – as lecturer, politician, playwright and journalist – had been lived through 'the most public media available'.[25] A cartoon in the *Western Mail* in May 1936 shows Lewis as a dandy, in a bow-tie and tailcoat, being held under the parish pump by the redoubtable Dame Wales. To one side of her stands the upright, handsome figure of a young man (looking rather too square-jawed and Teutonic for a native of Llŷn, it must be said) representing the unemployed, and to the other a confused but affable British government official, complete with trilby and clipboard. 'Give this lad of mine a job', Dame Wales tells the official, cocking a thumb at the young man, 'while I cool off this hothead'. There was no need to label Lewis in the cartoon: he had already won a reputation as a controversialist, especially so in his speeches. In an address to a fringe meeting at the National Eisteddfod in 1923 he had called for the formation of a Welsh battalion who would drill with wooden rifles under the command of a Welsh officer as an act of civil provocation.[26] Three years later, in his lecture *Egwyddorion Cenedlaetholdeb* ('The Principles of Nationalism'), delivered at the Welsh Nationalist Party's first summer school in Machynlleth, he had asserted that the party's greatest enemy was nationalism itself; and in 1929 told the Celtic Congress that the worshippers praying in ugly Nonconformist chapels 'bend down sitting as though they were vomiting. It is sadly appropriate'.[27]

When he addressed the jury in Caernarfon, then, his personal history virtually obliged him to say the unexpected – just as the circumstances made the act itself necessary. If Penyberth hadn't existed, Lewis would have had to invent it. Its site on the pilgrims'

route to Bardsey Island, its location in monoglot Welsh Wales, the
connections of the house (albeit in a minor way) with the tradition
of poetic patronage in the Middle Ages and the history of Owain
Glyndŵr, and the year in which it was pulled down – on the four-
hundredth anniversary of the Act of Union, 'an especial year of
affirmation',[28] as Lewis called it – made any other action
unthinkable. Some even read a symbolic significance into the date,
8 September. 'It was Our Lady's birthday night that the fire was
kindled, not by knowledge or design, but some there are who see
design in the fact which sets a seal upon its essential rightness.'[29]
The method chosen was redolent too: it was a fire to warm and
enlighten, to consume and destroy: a beacon, a Pentecost flame,
the light of a votive candle.

The Caernarfon speech is not a defence but a metanarrative. It
creates its effect not by flourishes or hyperbole but rather by what
rhetoricians would call its disposition, or the arrangement and
selection of its material. As in his 'Llygad y Dydd' poem, Lewis
builds in two directions: he works outwards: from the lecture
rooms in Swansea via nationalist politics, to Wales, to Britain, to
Europe and on to Armageddon; and as he does so he
simultaneously ascribes a symbolic significance to each step. He
begins with his personal history, establishing the correspondence
between action in time and impulse beyond time that echoes
through what follows. His work as a lecturer, he says, is both his
'professional duty' and his 'pride and delight': the literary tradition
he embraces draws its 'sustenance' from the living language and
demands that security and family be 'sacrificed' if it is to be
preserved. Sustenance, sacrifice and salvation – the trinity that
make sense of the symbols of the mass – are implicit in his next
assertion that it was the claims of literature 'that first led me from
purely literary work to public affairs and to the establishment of
the Welsh Nationalist Party'.[30] He chooses his example advisedly
when, as an example of practical politics he cites the scheme
established among the unemployed 'whereby on Thursday of
every week a man whose position in life is comfortable gives up
his dinner and sends the price of it to provide a three-course dinner
for an unemployed fellow-Welshman whose larder on Thursday is
empty'.[31]

Having established his bona fides as one who is prepared to make sacrifices, he turns to the specifics of the campaign, or the 'crusade' as he calls it. His 'argument in four stages' has the outward appearance of a logical and narrative development. With dates, statistics and quotations from correspondence and even a page reference from the anthology *Cynfeirdd Lleyn*, to a mid-sixteenth-century poem written at the farmhouse, Lewis outlines the 'horror' of his fellow-Welshmen at the establishment of the bombing range; the 'patience' and 'sacrifice' of 'legitimate persuasion' to the proposal; the government's indifference; and the act itself as an expression of 'the conflict of obedience' between state and the 'moral law' to which the three in the dock were driven.[32]

The events as Lewis narrates them, although scrupulously factual, only tell part of the story. A parallel yet contrary account exists. When the Air Ministry announced, as reported in the *Manchester Guardian* on 1 June 1935, that 'proposals are under consideration' to build a training school for bomber pilots at Porth Neigwl in Llŷn (it was one of Lewis's incidental symbolic triumphs that he brought 'Penyberth' – with its hint of 'aberth' or 'sacrifice' – into the discourse), the Welsh Nationalist Party hardly noticed it. True, the Caernarfonshire branch announced its opposition the following day, and Lewis himself announced in the party's executive in August, as the twelfth item on the agenda, that 'the matter is a very important one' and called on the Caernarfonshire branch to 'make propaganda out of it';[33] but it had no wider influence than that. The only public body to raise its voice against the development for the rest of the year was the forerunner of the Council for the Protection of Rural Wales. After all, the site in Wales was the fourth to be named, after successful campaigns in Abbotsbury, Dorset (where there were nesting swans), Holy Island, Northumberland (rare ducks) and Friskney in East Anglia (fishing grounds) had scuppered previous plans.

Lewis had predicted that 1935 would be a year of 'unbroken, monotonous, tiring work . . . heroism all the harder because of its day-in-day-out lack of romance',[34] and so it had proved. The year, like those throughout the 1930s, was taken up with the familiar battles for small concessions: an independent economic

development council, separate provision in broadcasting, the Welsh
language, dominion status, a Secretary of State and a capital city,
the recognition of Monmouthshire as a Welsh county. There were
tilts at the English popular press and valiant attempts to persuade
the membership that the general election in November (where the
party could not afford to field any candidates) was an irrelevance.
'I would give much to be able to free myself from the burden of
leading Plaid', he wrote to a friend that summer. 'I take no delight
in the post; only duty, unless I am deceiving myself woefully,
keeps me in it.'[35] As he faced 1936, the focus of his party's
national protest was its opposition to the arrival in Wales, for one
year only, of an agricultural show. The Bath and West had been
invited to Neath in the same year as the town hosted the National
Eisteddfod. He had spent half of 1934 and the whole of 1935 in a
flurry of activity to have the invitation withdrawn, resigning from
the Eisteddfod's board of adjudicators and lobbying others to do
the same. No one listened.

In his editorial for the party's monthly, *Y Ddraig Goch*, for
January 1936, written before Christmas, he looked back over the
previous ten years of the party's existence. 'Broadly speaking,' he
wrote, 'it can be said that these ten years have been ten years of
preparation.' He acknowledged that the party had made progress.
Its membership had grown year on year, it had established
branches, seen its share of the vote double in the local elections it
had fought, and Lewis himself estimated that he had addressed
several hundred meetings. It had all been 'tiring, hard and
monotonous work'. The party had become a talking-shop,
presenting 'crude, unconsidered motions' at conference, living on
words and appealing to the intellect when it was evident that the
appeal wasn't working. 'God preserve us from Plaid becoming
merely a party of elegant speechifiers.' In short, something needed
to be *done*. 'Let us continue to protest. Let us continue to
persuade. But it is high time now for us to progress from protest to
action.' He referred, among other things, to the threat to make 'the
Welsh areas of Llŷn into a practice ground for the hellish bombs of
the English' (the first time that Lewis has referred to the Bombing
School publicly as a threat about which something could be done)
and closed with this:

Let us begin the next ten years by showing that we shall consecrate not only our tongues to protect our country but our bodies too. Men of Wales, you, women of Wales, we are calling you to face mockery, hatred, derision and contempt – and a happy new year and a new period in the history of the Welsh Nationalist Party.[36]

His call was answered in an anonymous item in the *Western Mail* on the last day of 1935. Under the headline 'Welsh Nationalists Become Passive Resisters', the piece said that after ten years of 'ineffectual begging for Home Rule the principle of protest has already been ousted by the principle of action.' Its source was 'one prominent member of the Welsh Nationalist Party', 'Mr X', as the paper called him, who was quoted at length:

The time has come to do something, and if our bodies are broken or our lives forfeit what will it matter if the end is achieved? . . . I am urging Nationalists to go to Porth Neigwl and lay themselves across the road in front of the lorries taking building materials to the Air Station. They will challenge the drivers to take the lorries over their bodies.

There may be deaths. There will certainly be imprisonment. But it is only by martyring ourselves that we can arouse Wales to a sense of nationhood.[37]

Lewis had known nothing about the interview beforehand, or the identity and status of 'Mr X' – indeed, it wasn't certain that 'Mr X' existed. He could not contradict this anonymous call to martyrdom without showing weakness, ignorance or lack of leadership. He wrote to the party organizer J. E. Jones on the same day, unable to understand how his demand that Welshmen and women should give their bodies had been interpreted in this particular and extreme fashion: '. . . I thought that I had been quite non-committal and promised nothing'.[38] Jones replied by return of post that he believed Lewis Valentine, the party's vice-president at the time, to be 'Mr X' but that he was not completely sure.[39]

It is a telling illustration of the haphazard way in which the party operated. More importantly, it was the beginning of a frantic fortnight in which Lewis turned another man's outspokenness into an act upon which the rest of his own life would turn. Lewis wrote at length to Jones again on the same day that he received his answer – by which time the still anonymous speaker's outburst had been quoted in the *Manchester Guardian*: 'I do not condemn any of "Mr X's" suggestions in the *Western Mail*.' If it were indeed Valentine, the news was to be welcomed 'if this is a sign that he is taking a definite lead in the North'. The error, Lewis decided, was not the proposed act itself but that it had been announced in advance: '. . . public statements should come *after* action'. The next step was 'to go forward with care and determination to prepare'. He suggested that Jones should arrange for a deputation to visit the site and report on progress, suggested distributing propaganda 'from house to house in Llŷn to awaken the conscience', and undertook himself to 'give the matter prominence' in the next issue of *Y Ddraig Goch*. In the meantime he proposed 'holding meetings, not to protest to the government, but to prepare the country for an act of interference . . . *let none of us withdraw*.' He closed with a word of encouragement for the possible cause of the upset just three days before. 'Tell Valentine to press on now . . . And if some members are fearful and want to hold back, let Valentine know that he can say that it was my editorial that was chiefly responsible for the plan and that it is too late to withdraw without bringing shame on the party . . . "Mr X's" words in the *Western Mail* have taken the initiative from me, and we must now make Porth Neigwl the main object of our attack and the Bath & West a secondary issue.' What would follow, he added, would be 'the far harder trick of attacking Porth Neigwl and rousing the necessary spirit for that in the party.'[40]

A little over a week later something like a campaign was underway, run by a secret subcommittee of five appointed by Lewis himself from the other end of the country in Swansea. Letters were sent to Nonconformist ministers in the area on 13 January and the site was visited in the same week. Jones reported that 'no work has been started yet; it is unlikely that it will begin for a month or two.' It appeared, he continued, 'that the people who expected work and profit from the camp are beginning to doubt now whether they will get anything.'[41] Lewis, however, was not in the mood for the anticlimax of a successful campaign: 'The sound of the threats will begin to rise before long, I hope – and the blow . . . Gandhi's methods will not work there. The hangars must be burned down.' The whole process, from potential embarrassment to conviction, had taken under three weeks.[42]

This is not the story Lewis chose for his address, because his talk of thwarted reasonableness during the spring and summer of 1936 and the apparent gradual realization that another road would need to be taken is the necessary counterpoint to another story told in the latter half of his address: 'Thus ended peaceful persuasion along legitimate democratic lines', he says of the news that building work had begun in June. 'There only remained now the way of sacrifice.'[43] This second narrative effectively negates the name-dropping and numbers games he plays so sedulously in his account of the campaign itself: the 'seven or eight thousand people' who signalled their disapproval of the proposed development at the May rally in Pwllheli, chaired by 'the most eminent literary man in Wales, Professor W. J. Gruffydd',[44] the thousands who signed the petitions, the request for the Prime Minister to receive a deputation signed by 'twenty eminent Welsh leaders . . . the principals of Aberystwyth and of Bangor and of Bala-Bangor theological colleges, the secretary of the Honourable Society of Cymmrodorion, the Bishop of Menevia . . . '.[45] It rejustifies the arson by bringing it within 'the universal moral law (what we call in Welsh *y ddeddf foesol*) which is an essential part of Christian tradition and is recognized by moral theologians to be binding on all men'.[46] The parenthetical gloss is characteristic Saunders Lewis gamesmanship: '*y ddeddf foesol*' has no more currency or resonance in Welsh than its English equivalent; but its inclusion lends authority to what follows and makes obedience to the law appear to be a particularly Welsh virtue. The moral law, Lewis says, 'recognizes the family and the nation to be moral persons. They have the qualities and the natural rights of persons',[47] and therefore the act of the 'brute power of the state'[48] against the moral person of nation represents the broader desecration of Christian tradition, making its defence – and Lewis doesn't use the words lightly – 'a matter of life and death':

Now, everywhere in Europe today we see governments asserting that they are above the moral law of God, that they recognize no other law but the will of the government, and that they recognize no other power but the power of the state. These governments claim absolute powers;

they deny the rights of persons and of moral persons. They deny that
they can be challenged by any code of morals, and they demand the
absolute obedience of men. Now that is Atheism. It is the denial of
God, of God's law. It is the repudiation of the entire Christian tradition
of Europe, and the beginning of the reign of chaos.[49]

This second, metaphysical interpretation has the effect of
rendering the specifics of the Air Ministry's action and, indeed, the
arson itself immaterial. The English state's interference in Welsh
life was a grievance waiting for a symbol. The arson was an assault
on a known enemy; the speech dressed the assault in words.

Lewis's appeal to the Caernarfon jury delayed his imprisonment
until the new year. On 2 March 1937, the three men were given
special permission to leave their cells at Wormwood Scrubs to
listen to a broadcast of Lewis's radio play *Buchedd Garmon* ('The
Life of Germanus'), a story of the heroic defence of Christian
orthodoxy and commissioned by the BBC within a week of the
Caernarfon trial. It is a piece best known for one purple passage, a
speech since reproduced on posters and coffee cups, where Wales
is described as a vineyard given by God to the care of the Welsh,
to be protected against the pigs that rush in to trample it. As
significant, however, were the sentiments he ascribed to a
nameless character, 'one of the crowd':

> We are the common people.
> Our thoughts do not walk in the suppleness of words
> Like the reasoning of philosophers.
> Our thoughts take shape
> In earthenware vessels and wooden goods,
> In tackle and tools and the serving of meat and drink,
> In the taming of a horse or the fashioning of a cartwheel;
> The thoughts of the common people are obscure and sacramental
> Forcing their way from the mind through the hands into the
> stubborn mould of their needs.
> We are not easily deceived by handiwork, but we are readily
> snared by words.

Hearing the broadcast was a 'thrill'. A fortnight later he wrote to his
family that 'the reception was perfect, without interruption at all'.

NOTES

[1] For ease of reference, quotations and page references from the now rare *Why We Burnt the Bombing School* (Caernarfon, 1936) will be taken from Alun R. Jones and Gwyn Thomas (eds.), *Presenting Saunders Lewis* (2nd edition, Cardiff, 1983), 115–26.

[2] National Library of Wales, Lord Edmund-Davies papers, box 1. Lewis to Edmund Davies, 8 September 1976. Davies confirmed the story to Ivor Wynne Jones shortly before Lewis's death, *Liverpool Daily Post*, 16 April 1983: 'Saunders Lewis would not hear of it,' he wrote of the proposed defence, 'making it very clear that none of the three wanted to be found not guilty on a legal technicality.'

[3] Dafydd Glyn Jones, 'His Politics', in Alun R. Jones and Gwyn Thomas, *op. cit*, 66.

[4] Alun Talfan Davies, 'Ymadawiad y Brenin', *Barn*, 273 (1985), 365.

[5] J. E. Jones, *Tros Gymru* (Abertawe, 1970), 188.

[6] A. J. P. Taylor, 'Introduction' in Reginald Reynolds (ed.), *British Pamphleteers, volume two: from the French Revolution to the nineteen thirties* (London, 1951), 9.

[7] 'Sgwrs â Saunders Lewis', *Baner ac Amserau Cymru*, 23 December 1942.

[8] 'Celf Drama', *Y Darian*, 20 Mai 1920, 2.

[9] 'Celfyddyd y Ddrama', *Y Darian*, 27 May 1920, 1.

[10] 'Arluniaeth mewn Drama', *ibid*, 10 June 1920, 7.

[11] 'Y Briodas: Dehongliad', *Y Llenor*, 6 (Gaeaf 1927), 194.

[12] *Ibid.*, 200.

[13] *Williams Pantycelyn* (Llundain, 1927), 19.

[14] *Ibid.*, 20.

[15] 'Pasiant neu Sagrafen', *Baner ac Amserau Cymru*, 8 July 1926. Reprinted in Marged Dafydd (ed.), *Ati, Wŷr Ifainc: ysgrifau gan Saunders Lewis* (Caerdydd, 1986), 1–3.

[16] *Braslun o Hanes Llenyddiaeth Gymraeg* (Caerdydd, 1932), 21.

[17] *Braslun*, 64.

[18] *Braslun*, 69.

[19] 'The Essence of Welsh Literature', *Wales*, 7 (1947), 340–1.

[20] *Selected Poems: Saunders Lewis*, translated from the Welsh by Joseph P. Clancy (Cardiff, 1993), 1.

[21] *Selected Poems*, 2.

[22] 'Cenedlaetholdeb a Chyfalaf', *Y Ddraig Goch*, June 1926, 3. Reprinted in *Canlyn Arthur* (Aberystwyth, 1938), 16–17, from which all subsequent references are taken.

[23] 'Cenedlaetholdeb a Chyfalaf', 16–17.

[24] 'Cenedlaetholdeb a Chyfalaf', 20.

[25] Bobi Jones, 'Portread', *Barn*, 273 (1985), 369.

[26] 'Dyfodol y Mudiad Cenedlaethol', *Baner ac Amserau Cymru*, 9 August 1923.

[27] 'The Literary Man's Life in Wales', *Welsh Outlook*, 16 (October 1929), 295.

[28] '1536–1936', *The Welsh Nationalist*, June 1934.

[29] Frances Wynne, The True Level (Dublin, 1947), 86. Quoted in Hazel Walford Davies, *Saunders Lewis a Theatr Garthewin* (Llandysul, 1995), 27.

[30] *Presenting Saunders Lewis*, 115.

[31] *Ibid.*, 116.

[32] *Ibid.*, 117.

[33] NLW, Plaid Cymru papers, A27. Minutes of the Welsh Nationalist Party executive, 27 August 1935.

[34] 'Ymreolaeth ar Fater y Radio', *Y Ddraig Goch*, Ionawr 1935.

[35] NLW, Griffith John Williams papers, Lewis to Griffith John Williams, 11 July 1935

[36] 'Llywydd y Blaid yn Trafod ei Gorffennol a'i Dyfodol', *Y Ddraig Goch*, Ionawr 1936.

[37] *Western Mail*, 31 December 1935.

[38] NLW, Plaid Cymru papers B121. Lewis to J. E. Jones, 31 December 1935. Lewis's word translated here as 'non-committal' is 'cwestiynnol' [*sic*]: literally, 'questioning'.

[39] *Ibid.* J. E. Jones to Lewis, 1 January 1936.

[40] *Ibid.* Lewis to J. E. Jones, 2 January 1936.

[41] *Ibid.* J. E. Jones to Lewis, 18 January 1936.

[42] *Ibid.* Lewis to J. E. Jones, undated, but before 22 January 1936, when Jones wrote to Lewis Valentine, Plaid Cymru papers B121, quoting Lewis's words received 'the other day'.

[43] *Presenting Saunders Lewis*, 121.

[44] *Ibid.*, 120.

[45] *Ibid.*, 121.

[46] *Ibid.*, 122.

[47] *Ibid.*, 122.

[48] *Ibid.*, 124.

[49] *Ibid.*, 125.

[50] Mair Saunders Jones, Ned Thomas, Harri Pritchard Jones (eds.), *Saunders Lewis: letters* (Cardiff, 1993), 588. Lewis to 'Auntie Ellen', 15 March 1937.

WALDO WILLIAMS, 'IN TWO FIELDS', AND THE 38th PARALLEL

Damian Walford Davies

1. Fieldwork: The Ground of 'In Two Fields'

Ironically, it is perhaps the democratic inclusiveness of Waldo Williams's celebrated poem of 1956, 'Mewn Dau Gae' – 'In Two Fields' – that has rendered the poem 'difficult' for many readers (difficult enough, at any rate, to elicit a gloss from the poet: 'Had I known it was dark', he said, 'I would not have published it'[1]). Naturalization of paradox; *chiaroscuro* lighting effects; shifts between 'singular and plural, personal and collective', 'affirmative' and 'questioning' modes;[2] exhilarating expansions and stringent contractions of perspective that allow an insistent, even prosaic, localism to yield to the universal and visionary, which in turn funnel back down to *this* place and to history, newly apprehended – such techniques make 'In Two Fields' at once accessible and very demanding. (Of course, it is a poem about different kinds of 'access': to land, to history, to moments of vision, to other human beings.)

'In Two Fields' is a topographical poem that names the fields in question – Weun Parc y Blawd and Parc y Blawd – three times, boldly braving the pedestrian, knowingly negotiating what Michael Cronin has recently referred to as 'the romanticism of the particular'.[3] Considering the challenges of translation, Rowan Williams catches the effect succinctly: 'the names, either in English or Welsh, seem to me to hold up the poem in translation, giving a moment either exotic or banal'.[4] But the mirroring of the names strengthens our sense of the poem's investment in geographical precision – OS SN 126 203, for the record. It also has the important effect of acclimatizing us, through echo and

repetition, to the poem's governing aesthetics–politics of
difference-in-unity. (Fieldwork reveals that Parc y Blawd – 'Flour
Field' – as the name suggests, is a wheat field, while Weun Parc y
Blawd – 'Flour Moor Field' – is more marshy, suited to potato
crops and grazing.[5]) It is a religious poem (Quaker/ Baptist/
mystical/ apocalyptic/ millenarian); this most ecumenical[6] of poems
characteristically admits of various denominational readings (or
rather, asks us to dissolve the whole idea of denominationalism). It
is also a sort of Welsh *Prelude* in miniature, identifying the source
of the sustaining vision underlying Waldo's moral and political
outlook in the revelation of universal brotherhood he experienced
as a teenager in 1917 or 1918 in the gap between two fields in
Carmarthenshire (*not* Pembrokeshire, as has always been assumed
– a fact that should make us attend more carefully to the poem's
interest in boundaries):

> Weun Parc y Blawd and Parc y Blawd are two fields on the land of a
> friend and old neighbour of mine, John Beynon, Y Cross, Clunderwen.
> In the gap between the two fields about forty years ago, I realised
> suddenly and very vitally, in a personal circumstance of great
> definition, that men are, above all, brothers.[7]

We should remind ourselves, however, that for Waldo in the
summer of 1956, the poem was first and foremost a protest poem
and political intervention. Too often read as univocally celebratory
and affirmative, the poem is a troubled pastoral.

To those familiar with the poem but unfamiliar with Waldo's
comments on it, this may well come as a surprise, since 'In Two
Fields' cannot be said to flaunt its political credentials. Its location
in Waldo's single collection, *Dail Pren* (*Leaves of a Tree*, 1956),
between a poem of 1942 that homes in on the hellish presence of
the Arms Depot at Trecŵn ('Ar Weun Cas' Mael' – 'On
Puncheston Common') and a poem protesting against the
requisitioning of the Castlemartin Peninsula as a Tank Range by
the War Office in 1939 ('Daw'r Wennol yn Ôl i'w Nyth' – 'The
Swallow will Return to its Nest') should alert us to the fact that it
is no pastoral-mystical interlude. Moreover, its great political
prose co-texts of Waldo's *annus mirabilis* of 1956 – 'Brenhiniaeth

a Brawdoliaeth' ('Sovereignty and Brotherhood') and 'Pam y Gwrthodais Dalu Treth yr Incwm' ('Why I Refused to Pay the Income Tax') – together with Waldo's gloss on the poem and other documents confirm that the ground of 'In Two Fields' is Waldo's anarchism and pacifism, and that the poem is an imaginative inscription of the campaign he was waging throughout the 1950s against conscription, war, imperial possession and the superpower State. That campaign led, of course, to imprisonment in 1960 and 1961.

My aim in this essay is to scrutinize the poem's manifest and latent idiom of dissent and bring 'In Two Fields' into focus as a poem of the twentieth century's 'forgotten' war in Korea (1950-3) and as a response to the 1950s conflict in Cyprus. Seeking to recover the poem's historicity serves also to recover the relegated narratives of these tragedies. The war in Korea has too frequently been read as 'a footnote or as a prelude to engagements that have much deeper and more intense cultural penetration', such as the Second World War and Vietnam.[8] W. D. Erhart and Philip K. Jason recently noted that 'With scant attention by anthologists and critics, it's no wonder that the prevailing view is that few, if any, writers had their imaginations sparked by the war in Korea'.[9] It is hoped that this essay's engagement with 'In Two Fields' will contribute not only to the current retrieval and serious critical assessment of this neglected body of literature, but also to our understanding of the ways in which a poet might choose to write war.[10]

Previous discussions have valuably gestured at the way in which 'In Two Fields' is keyed into conflict, but they have tended to elide the complex vocality of the poem's war idiom by privileging its spiritual, apocalyptic or broad cultural dimensions.[11] The historicity of 'In Two Fields' deserves more sustained consideration. Taking as its ground two fields that are in many ways one, the poem is a politicized meditation on space and the (psycho-)topography of unity and division. We need to be reminded of the precise political significance of this terrain in the context of the 1950s. This essay therefore excavates the poem's geographical contours to suggest that 'In Two Fields' maps the international conflicts of the 1950s – Korea, Cyprus – in order to

project a new world geography, a unificatory, redemptive
geopolitics. This act of imagining is in line both with Waldo's
stated hope that *Dail Pren* would be 'a practical help to my nation
in the confusion of this age'[12] and with the biblical resonance of
the title of his volume, which is a phrase firmly rooted in 'In Two
Fields': 'the leaves of the tree [of life] were for the healing of the
nations' (*Revelation* 22:2).[13] Pennar Davies gave a sense of poem-
as-ground when he remarked of 'In Two Fields': 'Cân ydyw y
gellir byw ynddi ac arni' – 'It is a poem one can live in and on' –
while Hugh Bevan noted that Waldo's is a poetry 'of the open
field'.[14] Referring to 'In Two Fields', Rowan Williams speaks of
the ability of the alert translator to 'trace [Waldo's] movement
across a territory of perception and feeling'. I want to deepen our
sense of the poem's space by theorizing 'In Two Fields' around the
concept of ground and offering a reading of the poem as political
cartography.

Various translations of the poem are interesting in this regard.
Translation itself can usefully be considered an idiom of dissent
(more properly, perhaps, an idiom of dissenting assent, or
assenting dissent), and I want to scrutinize what happens to
Waldo's idiom during the process of translation. How have various
translators encountered 'In Two Fields', and in what forms has its
idiom of dissent survived conscription into another (Waldo's
mother-) tongue? Of particular interest here is the way in which
these translations – each a critical reading of sorts, as commentators
have noted[15] – can be seen to focus, amplify or diffuse the political
discourse of the original. Appropriately, translating 'In Two Fields'
gives the reader access to two cultural fields; it is an act of doubling
in tune with the spirit (and indeed anxieties) of the original.[16]

'[Waldo's] whole work', says Tony Conran, 'is a protest against
violence':

> [O]f all the possible attitudes to armed conflict that poets can take –
> Rupert Brooke, Edward Thomas, Wilfred Owen, David Jones, Alun
> Lewis, Sorley MacLean – his is the most extreme in its opposition'.[17]

It would be useful to chart the trajectory of that dissent. A mixture
of inheritance and insight went into the making of Waldo's

pacifism, anti-imperialism, 'necessary anarchism' and nationalism.[18] The seeds were sown early in a radicalized home. The basic tenets of the Quakerism he would formally embrace in the 1950s – pacifism foremost among them – were part of his Baptist heritage, as Waldo gratefully acknowledged in his Quaker declaration of faith in 1956. From his father, J. Edwal Williams, and his uncle, William Williams ('Gwilamus'), he inherited a pathological hatred of militarism and imperialism. His principles were also moulded in significant ways by his mother, Angharad, and by his sisters (the death of his sister Morvydd in 1915 provides us with another context for the instressed vision at the heart of 'In Two Fields'). The poem bearing his mother's name in *Dail Pren* ascribes to her the very characteristics and values evident in Waldo's mature poetry and acts of protest: the capacity imaginatively to apprehend, and empathize with, the plight of others; a willingness to privilege actions over mere words; and a conception of interpersonal relationships and literary creativity as redemptive and healing. Conran has (rightly) identified in Waldo's poetry a strong alignment with the feminine – 'His mother, his sisters and his wife are quite crucially involved both in his greatness as a poet, and in the political reality he represents'.[19] That alignment functions as a mode of opposition to masculine violence and imperialist aggression.

His experience in the liminal, littoral space ('These two fields a green sea-shore . . . ', as Rowan Williams translates the opening line[20]) between two ordinary fields during the Great War confirmed these intuitions, and was to serve as a lifelong touchstone. The wartime context of that initial vision is telling.[21] Detaching that sudden apprehension of fundamental unity from its historical moment (as critics have tended to do) detracts from its full import as a revelation in part motivated by war and issuing ultimately in social and political action. (A corollary of this, and the ground of this essay, is that 'In Two Fields', which recalls that experience and reimagines it in the context of another war, represents a fertile field for historicist analysis.) Though that vision had to wait forty years to achieve literary expression, the fields served as a site of dissent throughout Waldo's career – an oppositional topography, representing a furiously pacifist alternative to the innumerable killing fields of the twentieth century.[22]

From 1923 to 1927, Waldo's moral and political allegiances took on intellectual vigour and gained a social dimension at the University College of Wales, Aberystwyth, as his early works of polemical prose demonstrate. The nature and scope of his pacifist radicalism were crystallized by the violence of the Second World War, which also laid bare for him the insidious means by which the modern State (nominally democratic as well as overtly totalitarian) violated the sacrosanct freedom of the individual – conscription being for Waldo one of the most pernicious examples. His first public, political poem, 'Y Tŵr a'r Graig' – 'The Tower and the Rock' (1938), in which the primeval and medieval are invested with contemporary political resonance – was motivated by Lord Strabolgi's proposal in the House of Lords in November 1938 that 'some measures of compulsory service' in the armed forces be adopted as conflict with Germany loomed. The Second World War was in part responsible for a phobic vision of poisoned soil and ultra-violent Darwinian nature that paralysed Waldo for sixth months from 1939 to 1940 and which he dramatized in the nightmarish surreality of 'O Bridd' ('O Soil of the Earth').[23] To be grounded at this time was to be wholly incapacitated. His recovery and reconciliation with the soil yielded – indeed, made possible – war poems of astringent clarity: 'Look: bodies of children. Dead at nightfall/ . . . White and black and yellow. A multitude' ('Y Plant Marw'/ 'The Dead Children'). (Waldo Williams is Welsh literature's most ruthless deployer of periods and staccato[24] notation; the groundwork of his punctuation is a vital aspect of his idiom of dissent.) His uncompromising pacifist stance, articulated in a series of letters to the *Western Telegraph* in 1939 and 1940, resulted in tension with the county's Director of Education that made his position as headmaster of Puncheston primary school untenable.[25] Summoned before a conscientious objectors' tribunal in Carmarthen in February 1942, Waldo the absolutist delivered his remarkable pacifist 'Statement': war, which 'starves to death the innocence of the world', is a 'monstrous violation' of 'the Divine Imagination which brought forth the world'.[26] (The idiom, of course, invokes the witness of that arch-dissenter and 'prophet against empire', William Blake.) The death of his wife Linda in 1943 after barely two years of marriage deepened his personal trauma at a time of international crisis, and he embarked on a voluntary five-year 'exile' in England that both sharpened his sense of dislocation and afforded him a salutary new perspective on a Wales threatened by increasing anglicization and by the depredations of a War Office hungry for land.[27]

But if it was the Second World War that motivated him to clarify and conceptualize his pacifism, it was the Korean War that defined and mobilized it. Waldo returned to Wales in 1949. That partial regrounding meant that he would insist on locating and formulating his opposition to war and military conscription in the context of Wales's relation to Britain and to the international community. A politics of home intersected with an internationalist vision; Waldo's outlook anticipates that contemporary programme of 'think global, act local'.[28] Korea compelled him to privilege actions over words, protest over poetry. Only then could he allow himself the luxury (as he saw it) of protest poetry. Indeed, to speak of Waldo's idiom of dissent in the 1950s runs the risk of missing the point entirely. As he explained in June 1956 to his friends J. Gwyn Griffiths and Kate Bosse-Griffiths (the former, in response to Waldo's perceived inertia regarding the publication of his poems, having assembled a collection that actually reached proof stage before the poet himself intervened): 'I must say that it is not shyness that has kept me from publishing, but my criticism of this age, this civilization, and this country in particular. Too many words, not enough actions'. And to D. J. Williams in October of that year: 'when the Korean War came, you know how I felt about my peace poems. I felt that to bring them together in a book would be awful, hypocritical, unbearable, if I did not try to do something other than merely write about this thing'.[29] It was an example of what one commentator has termed Waldo's 'terrifying sincerity'.[30] He resigned his teaching post and began a decade-long campaign of civil disobedience by withholding his income tax. In the circumstances of the early 1950s, then, action was the primary, obligatory idiom of dissent. Each subsequent utterance in poetry and polemical prose was performative.

2. Korea and Cyprus, Conscription and Division

What issues, then, did the Korean War throw into relief for Waldo Williams? Korea plays a central, illustrative role in his two great prose polemics of summer 1956, 'Sovereignty and Brotherhood' and 'Why I Refused to Pay the Income Tax', which hinge on 'In Two Fields' to form a remarkable summer triptych of dissent. These two pieces help establish the political ground of 'In Two Fields'. (The July 1956 radio broadcast, 'Paham yr Wyf yn Grynwr' – 'Why I am a Quaker' – can be considered a pendant to these.) The concerns of the political prose pieces are emphatically those of 'In Two Fields'; Ned Thomas is right to say that 'Why I Refused to Pay the Income Tax' functions as 'an extended gloss' on 'In Two Fields', while Dafydd Elis Thomas recognizes that, by the same token, 'In Two Fields' can be read as 'a pacifist anti-conscription pamphlet'.[31]

'Sovereignty and Brotherhood', initially delivered as an address to the Peace Society at the Welsh Baptist Union conference in May 1956, is Waldo's great Berdyaev-influenced anarchist critique of individuals' unthinking acceptance of the authority of the modern State and of the ways in which the 'compulsory element' sustaining the State's traditional hegemony is internalized by its citizens. Korea is invoked as a prime illustration of the argument. Waldo begins by emphasizing the division of Korea, which 'laid her open to recrimination on both sides', and goes on to lament the way in which 'the United Nations was rushed to war by the United States in a paroxysm lest the chance be lost'. Citing reports detailing war atrocities, Waldo confronts the effects of violence both on human bodies – the hideous deformities caused by napalm bombs, the herding together and burning alive of civilians in a barn – and on the very ground of fractured Korea: 'The countryside was made desolate, the cities reduced to rubble and millions made homeless'. Taking to task his generation's apathy and lack of collective responsibility regarding Korea and the acts of violence perpetrated 'in our name and on our behalf', Waldo asks:

> Was it because Korea was so distant? . . . Because the cruelty of our age had weakened our capacity to feel – or worse, had bred in us an

unacknowledged craving for excitement? . . . Or because we felt that the complexity of international politics had become too great for us to solve?[32]

The result, he contends, was a heightened, enervating dependence on the State, or rather on a false 'image' of it, constructed out of weakness and ignorance. Waldo concludes with an impassioned attack on the 'acme of Sovereignty's violence and the most perfect expression of the illogicality of the tradition that has perverted our nature and dimmed our sight': military conscription. 'Why I Refused to Pay the Income Tax', published in *Baner ac Amserau Cymru* on 20 June 1956 – exactly a week after 'In Two Fields' had appeared in the same newspaper – opens with the division of Korea. The contention that the United States 'got their way in the United Nations Conference – through deception' and 'rushed the United Nations to war' is reiterated,[33] and the holocaustal horrors detailed in 'Sovereignty and Brotherhood' are revisited: 'I felt that Korea was our own Belsen. The Belsen of America and England and Wales'. A section headed 'Conscription' boldly configures a pacifist, nationalist and republican argument along a Wales–Korea axis, emphasizing Wales's enforced complicity in the State's imperial projects in Korea from 1950 to 1953, and, at the moment of writing, in Cyprus. Refusing to allow distance (geographical, chronological) to blur unignorable adjacency (a project in which 'In Two Fields' is also involved), Waldo reminded his readers that 'some of our young lads were being compelled to go over to assist in the wickedness' in Korea, and challenged them with a radical fore-shortening of contemporary geopolitical perspectives. The Conscription Act meant that the Korean War 'in its worst, executive aspect' had 'taken over the homes of Wales'. Waldo's formulation functions as a pacifist, nationalist subversion of Prime Minister Clement Attlee's famous statement in a broadcast of 31 July 1950 justifying British involvement in Korea through an alarmist telescoping:

> If the aggressor gets away with it, aggressors all over the world will be encouraged. The same results which led to the second world war will follow . . . The fire that has been started in distant Korea may burn down your house.[34]

Waldo's pacifist, transnationalist, anti-imperialist logic insistently maps a divided Korea onto Wales, a compromised Wales onto Korea, just as it seeks to replace a sense of what Waldo called 'vicarious guilt' regarding 'the horrors of Korea' with an awareness of 'personal guilt' so incapacitating that he found 'going out into the street' an ordeal. 'Military conscription imprisons me completely', he said.[35]

Waldo's 1958 gloss on 'In Two Fields' unequivocally signals the poem's historical embeddedness and political agenda. The 'Exiled King' of the poem (indebted to George William Russell's 'outlawed majesty'), walking 'through some crisis in history', is revealed to be the opponent of 'the powers that possess the world'. Towards the end of the gloss, Waldo quotes another poem of his in which the two fields, through the suggestive logic of apposition, become the grounding geography of pacifist resistance and opposition: 'Weun Parc y Blawd and Parc y Blawd/ Summer's long song will return./ Pledge my hand to the cruel sword/ I never did, and never will'. The gloss concludes with a striking statement of the poem's political meaning:

> For me, the main message of this poem, 'In Two Fields', in terms of the contemporary moment, is that the Welch Regiment is in Cyprus still, and so long as we tolerate military conscription, they are our slaves. What shall we do? That is why I wanted to explain the poem.[36]

That position was echoed in private correspondence. 'If my nephew Dafydd, for example, were in the army and in Cyprus or some other place', Waldo told J. Gwyn Griffiths and Kate Bosse-Griffiths in 1956, six days after the publication of 'In Two Fields' and a day before the appearance of 'Why I Refused to Pay the Income Tax', 'seeing all my propaganda collected in a book, and that book praised by people, would just increase the bitterness'.[37] 'Propaganda' is interesting here: a troubled acknowledgement that words are not to be trusted unless legitimized by correlative action.

Significantly, Waldo's wider critique of the modern State is articulated in terms of the division at the heart of modern Korea's historical narrative. In 'Why I Refused to Pay the Income Tax', he cites a moment of anarchist clarity when the State's 'awful dualism' – its internal structural 'order' and the 'chaos' subsisting between it and the world – was revealed. For Waldo, the split was replicated in the moral fracture forced upon subjects who accept the evils of the State in return for the benefits of citizenship. It was from this psychological rift, ethical paradox or double-bind, and unbridgeable division, that Waldo sought to free himself by refusing to pay his Income Tax.

'In Two Fields' is painfully alive to such dualities. Its map of Welsh ground, both demarcated and imaginatively unified, was drawn from contemporary history. Since the late nineteenth century, Korea had been the victim of the shifting dynamics of imperial rivalry between China, Russia and Japan. From 1910 to 1945, it was subject to often draconian Japanese colonial rule, unsuccessfully resisted by various Korean nationalist factions. The defeat of Japan in 1945 resulted not in the independence of a unified Korea but in the division of the country (superpower trusteeship and 'murderous' Korean political factionalism both playing a part)[38] along the 38th Parallel (the 38 degrees north parallel of latitude), demarcating the North (where the defeated Japanese surrendered to Soviet forces) from the South (where Japan surrendered to the United States). The 38th Parallel – a 'rough and ready division'[39] chosen in half an hour by two young colonels, Rusk and Bonesteel, using a crude National Geographic map – was very quickly sealed by the Communist North, and the two occupation zones, under American military authority and Korean Communist control, swiftly hardened into ideological opposition. Attempts by the US and the United Nations to initiate Korea-wide elections failed; by 1948, the Republic of Korea and the Democratic People's Republic of Korea confronted each other over a tense, arbitrary line of latitude. On 25 June 1950, following guerrilla activity on both sides, Soviet-sponsored North Korean troops launched an offensive across the 38th Parallel, precipitating a war (officially and euphemistically designated a 'police action' by the West) that resulted in around four million casualties; two million of these were civilian deaths. The international community – Britain included – was drawn into the conflict after the United Nations Security Council ratified President Truman's call to resist Communist belligerence in the peninsula.[40] For Waldo, the British

State, faced with a chronic dearth of available troops, was visiting that belligerence on its Welsh citizens by means of the 'compulsory element' – delaying the release of regular soldiers 'whose contractual term of active duty had expired'; recalling reservists to full-time duty in the 'first rotation of battalions' sent out with the 29th Brigade; and compelling National Servicemen (whose obligatory service was increased from eighteen months to two years in 1950 in direct response to the Korean War) to fight in Korea.[41] By 1952, 'two-thirds at least of battalions were composed of National Servicemen'.[42] Throughout the war, and especially from spring 1951 to the Armistice of July 1953, when UN–US forces fought a holding action around it, the deadly rubicon of the 38th Parallel served as a potent symbol of political difference resulting in the horrors of modern war. The Armistice (without reunification) realigned and fortified the border along a Military Demarcation Line (MDL) buffered by a 'no man's land' Demilitarized Zone (DMZ) intersecting the 38th Parallel roughly south-west to north-east, along what had been the stalemate, 'ground-contact' battle-line. I suggest that 'In Two Fields' is concerned to map the dynamics of that conflict.

Colonial superintendence, thwarted unity, partition and violence: these are also the master-themes of the contemporary conflict in Cyprus, which, as Waldo's gloss makes clear, is at the heart of the anti-conscription agenda of 'In Two Fields'. Frustration with British colonial rule in the aftermath of the Second World War led in the early 1950s to an intensification of Greek Cypriot aspiration for *enosis* (union) with Greece. Such a campaign naturally increased tensions between the majority Greek Cypriot community and Turkish Cypriots. The formation of the National Organisation of Cypriot Fighters (EOKA) heralded in 1955 a campaign of guerrilla terrorist violence against British troops (a significant number of them conscripts) aimed at securing *enosis*. The year of 'In Two Fields', 1956, saw a massive increase in the number of British troops on Cyprus (HQ Middle East Command had already been moved there from Egypt in 1954); the Welch Regiment arrived in 1957 and did not leave until 1961. Partition was mooted by the Turkish community in 1958, the year of the gloss on 'In Two Fields', and violence (intercommunal as well as anti-British) continued throughout the 1950s until an independent Republic of Cyprus with a 'bicommunal' constitution came into being in 1960 (the year conscription was abolished in the UK). Practically speaking, such power-sharing-by-ethnic-quota manifested itself in tense division rather than in plurality-within-unity. During the 1960s, Turkish Cypriot nationalism and continued Greek Cypriot demands for *enosis* resulted in further violence and segregation (along the 'Green Line', for example, in the city of Nicosia) and in actual partition in 1974 along the 'Attila line' with its UN buffer-zone – the inevitable legacy of the discord of the 1950s.[43]

The drama of 'In Two Fields' is played out against these two 1950s narratives of divided Korean and Cypriot fields, with the poem's authentic particularism mediating a fraught awareness of Wales's enforced participation in these two international conflicts. Shadowing the modern meaning of 'conscription' are the older senses of 'putting in writing', 'writing down together', 'a conjoint signature'. Waldo's aversion to war and to the tyranny of the call-up in the summer of 1956 is an act of literary inscription in which personal and public history, Wales, Korea and Cyprus, make a fascinating conjoint signature.

3. The Idiom of Dissent/ Dissenting Assent, Assenting Dissent

Locating the co-texts and contexts of 'In Two Fields' enables us to recognize the poem as a layered utterance in which a celebratory vision is haunted by 'tremor[s] of anxiety' – a term used by Nicholas Roe to describe comparable sites of disturbance in Romantic lyrics that seem on the surface to be untroubled by the pressures of history.[44] 'In Two Fields' evinces what one might call a textual post-traumatic stress disorder. The poem-video of 'In Two Fields' included in the film *Dal Yma/ Nawr* (2004) suggests this 'layering' by choosing as its visual field the 2002 National Eisteddfod and its surrounding site – the disused airfield at St Davids, Pembrokeshire, built in 1943 for the Halifax bombers of Royal Air Force Coastal Command. The video offers a sense of the poem as geographical, chronological and conceptual palimpsest:

shots of the Eisteddfod field are interspersed with images of the wider airfield, where the concrete runways are returning to grassland and heathland. The eisteddfod's 'fair field full of folk' (a phrase from Langland's thoroughly politicized *Piers Plowman* evoked by Waldo in *y perci llawn pobl* at the end of his poem) is disturbed by traces of past violence. Referring to the Castlemartin Tank Range in the poem adjacent to 'In Two Fields' in *Dail Pren*, Waldo declares that 'war has come/ To rip the field of Crug y Mêl'. In more indirect and nuanced ways, 'In Two Fields', with its interest in palimpsestic mapping, presents Weun Parc y Blawd and Parc y Blawd as also 'ripped' by war.

The literal borderland status of Waldo's two fields should be emphasized, since the poem is concerned with problems of adjacency, gaps, boundary conditions and disputable space. Waldo would have been aware that the ground of his teenage vision was frontier land (literal, imaginative). Until the recent realignment of the county boundaries, the parish of Llandysilio was divided in two by the Pembrokeshire-Carmarthenshire border, with Weun Parc y Blawd and Parc y Blawd in the latter county, a matter of yards from the boundary.[45] The Landsker line – that linguistic border dividing the Pembrokeshire Welshry and Englishry – is also close by, exerting its own pressures, reminding Waldo of his own geographical and cultural trajectory.[46] The canonization in Welsh literature of 'In Two Fields' as the ultimate inscription of Waldo-as-and-in-Pembrokeshire is a choice example of the way in which we can mistake the ground of a poem – and thus a poet's position. It was only in 2002 that a Local Government Boundary Commission ceded the two fields (peacefully) to Pembrokeshire.[47] Does it matter? I suggest it does, when the poem under discussion is one that underscores the fundamental artificiality and virtuality of all 'enforced' borders.

The very title of Waldo's poem announces a desire to disturb and reconfigure geographies. By asking us to entertain a paradox, it invites us to inflect our sense of the ways in which ground might be inhabited, territory occupied, dividing 'Parallels' imposed and patrolled. How, precisely, can one be in two fields simultaneously? The title suggests a dissolution of separateness into oneness ('in' works hard here), but the idea of doubleness and its dark reflex –

disconnection – cannot be dispelled. Indeed, the poem is a space in which this imaginative, unificatory tenancy of the fields contends with an awareness of geographical demarcation and limit – a territory in which erased frontiers threaten to materialize back into Attila lines, and 'mass hypnosis' (Waldo's term, via Berdyaev) threatens to shut down the counter-intuitive thinking of dissent.[48] Seven translations of Waldo's poem – respectively by Tony Conran, R. M. Jones, R. Gerallt Jones, Gwyn Jones, Joseph Clancy, R. S. Thomas, and Rowan Williams – are known to me.[49] Only one translator dissents from the title 'In Two Fields'. Rowan Williams's fine rendering of the poem – a creative negotiation or 'free translation' rather than 'a crib to the Welsh'[50] – carries the title 'Between Two Fields'. It is an interesting inflection which, I suggest, registers the translator's sense of the disturbances of the poem. As a title, 'Between Two Fields' hints at a sense of division, liminality, border habitation and threshold possibility at which the poem itself worries away, whereas 'In Two Fields', though troubled, more confidently asserts a desire for synthesis. (Here, one might say of all good translations that they resist 'conscription' – that they conscientiously object to being slavishly 'drafted', in all senses, by the original.)

Traversing the gaps between the poem's six stanza-fields involves crossing borders. The boundary space between the first and second stanzas is a particularly important one. In Conran's translation: 'The great quiet he brought me.// Excitement he gave me'. With no verbal checkpoint, no preparatory briefing, the reader crosses no man's land, moving abruptly from one state/ State into another very different one, to find that they are part of one whole. Two truths straddle perimeter space; difference is celebrated and paradox naturalized at the moment a boundary is negotiated and therefore negated. Totality lies the other side of a border. Such formal effects are part of the poem's idiom of dissent. By enjambing the final line of stanza one (the only example of such a move in his, or any other, translation), Rowan Williams dispenses altogether with end-stopped Demarcation Lines (as at Korea's 38th Parallel), radically opening the stanza border and shepherding us through the buffer zone, carrying a portion of one field into the next:

One and the same the lightning
hunter across the field . . .
        . . . who from the vaults
above the bright-voiced whistlers, the keen darting plovers,
brought down on me such quiet, such

Quiet, enough to rouse me.

To enjamb is to 'stride', to 'encroach' – peaceably, here, into unknown territory. What emerges in different ways from the original and the translation is a sense of the permeability of all textual and national borders.

The poem is shot through with the discourse and imagery of war, conscripted here in the service of pacifist dissent. Waldo's agent of unification and reconciliation, the 'Exiled King', appears in martial guise throughout, waging guerrilla war against what Waldo called 'the powers that possess the world'. He appears in the first stanza as a *saethwr* and *heliwr*. Translators of the poem have used either 'hunter' or 'huntsman' for the latter. The rendering of *saethwr* is more interesting since different translations create markedly different effects. While Gwyn Jones, R. Gerallt Jones and Joseph Clancy have 'archer', and R. S. Thomas has 'bowman', Tony Conran, R. M. Jones and Rowan Williams choose 'marksman' – a term more attuned to the poem's contemporary resonance than the other phrases, which run the risk of momentarily archaizing a poem that is painfully aware of the meaning of total war and of the effects of atom and napalm bombs. In stanza five, the unifier is a *dihangwr o'r byddinoedd* – in R. S. Thomas's translation, a 'deserter from the world's armies' (as was Waldo himself in the eyes of the State throughout the 1950s). Thomas's line appropriately suggests that he is a fugitive from 'multinational' UN 'police action' forces as well as from all sovereign armies. Rowan Williams opts for a more expansive rendering: 'Who was it then . . . / . . . slipping past all our recruiting sergeants?'. The figure of the recruiting sergeant – introduced, Williams explains, as a divisive 'shadowy counterforce . . . who tries to seduce in an opposite direction, or tries to "conscript" the transcendent liberator into human service' – is an inspired choice since it works to assert the poem's primary anti-

conscription campaign. 'I think that's just about defensible
licence', Williams continues ('defensible' itself being an interesting
choice here), 'given that we do speak of "conscripting" ideas for
our purposes'.[51]

It is Rowan Williams who brings out the 'shadowy counterforce'
to Waldo's mystical pastoral in the fourth line of stanza two: *Y
brwyn lu yn breuddwydio'r wybren las* – 'the many rushes
dreaming the blue sky' (R. Gerallt Jones and R. S. Thomas). No
one could fault Jones or Thomas for their translations of *llu* here,
but Williams's version works harder, bringing out the darker
contours of Waldo's vocabulary and topography by choosing 'the
army of dozy rushes'. ('You are always looking or listening for
what these particular words in one language make possible, for
their range and echoes', Williams remarks; 'you are feeling around
them, sensing the alternatives they hint at and deny'.[52]) Other
translators opt for the middle ground of 'host of rushes', which
rather hovers between an acknowledgement of violence and a
willingness to dilute the contemporary force of the poem's
discourse. Conran has the self-consciously poetic 'hosting of
rushes'. This is something of a surprise, given that his translation
of the previous line, *Yr eithin aeddfed ar y cloddiau'n clecian*,
registers Waldo's *cloddiau* ('hedgerows') as 'escarpments' (whose
primary sense is military, not topographical), no doubt motivated
by the image of gorse 'crackling' with tiny seed-pod detonations in
the heat.

The next lines in stanza two, *Pwy sydd yn galw pan fo'r
dychymyg yn dihuno?/ Cyfod, cerdd, dawnsia, wele'r bydysawd* –
'When the imagination wakens, who calls/ Risc up and walk,
dance, look at the world?' (Conran) – is clearly a reference to the
exiled unifier. But the poem's co-texts ask us here to tune into
another call – that of the State – whose 'Call-up' in the 1950s
compelled eighteen-year-olds to 'Rise up' at the very moment the
imagination 'wakened' into maturity, and to engage in combat, if
necessary, at nineteen. The 'counterforce' is here again, as 'In Two
Fields' warns against all State interpellation, all institutionalized
'hailing'. All translators have 'call' here except Rowan Williams,
who chooses 'Someone is shouting'/ (who?)', which anticipates
his 'recruiting sergeant' of stanza five.

The poem's uneasy pastoral is again disturbed at the beginning of stanza three in the image of the *cymylau mawr ffoadur a phererin* – 'the big clouds, the fugitive pilgrims' (Conran), 'the great fugitive and pilgrim clouds' (Clancy). *Ffoadur* here is the word to watch; in the context of the poem's cumulative war discourse, 'fugitive' (chosen by six out of seven translators) seems to me a romanticization, a demobilization of the idiom of dissent that blunts its political sharpness. Rowan Williams foregrounds the meaning that was surely primary in Waldo's mind here: 'Clouds: big clouds, pilgrims, refugees'. Foremost in his mind, I suggest, since in 'Sovereignty and Brotherhood' Waldo makes a point of referring to the five million refugees of the Korean War. He would also have known that the conflict in Cyprus made one-third of the population homeless.[53] For Waldo in 1956, 'DP' stood not only for *Dail Pren* but also for 'Displaced Persons'. Moreover, the idiom of dissent in the image of the fugitive-refugee-pilgrim clouds (tinged with the late sun of a stormy November, in which Ned Thomas detects the 'blood of the Somme'[54]) is strengthened by allusion. Gwyn Thomas has suggested that *ffoadur a phererin* echoes a line from T. S. Eliot's *Little Gidding*, the fourth section of *Four Quartets* and one of the greatest war poems of the twentieth century in English: 'the spirit *unappeased and peregrine*/ Between two worlds become much like each other' (my emphasis).[55] One can see how 'unappeased and peregrine' might have suggested *ffoadur a phererin* – 'peregrine' itself containing a sense of both Welsh words and morphing into *pererin* over the linguistic border. The allusion deserves further exploration. Eliot's line occurs in the middle of the famous passage describing the speaker's meeting with the 'familiar compound ghost' at 'the uncertain hour before morning' during the London Blitz, as the smoke from bombed buildings rises into the sky, 'After the dark dove with the flickering tongue/ Had passed below the horizon of his homing'. The allusion carries into 'In Two Fields' not only the violence of a previous war but also the uncanniness of a liminal encounter in which compound identities meet on the same ground and 'compel' a 'recognition' (compare Waldo's later formulation *adnabod nes bod adnabod* – in Gwyn Jones's translation, 'recognition that asks recognition').

At the centre of stanza three is this territory's 38th Parallel: the hedge of ashtrees and maple separating Weun Parc y Blawd from its brother field, Parc y Blawd: *Lawr yn yr ynn a'r masarn a rannai'r meysydd* – 'Down where the ashtrees and maples divided the fields' (Conran). It is the poem's central image of division. Ned Thomas hears in the Welsh line 'an iron tone', remarking: 'If it was in a *gap* between two fields that Waldo experienced a sense that men were brothers, shouldn't we read "divide" as a negative term?'.[56] It is here that the (borderland) Carmarthenshire fields map North and South Korea and proleptically chart a divided Cyprus; it is here that the ashtrees and maple map Korea's Military Demarcation Line and Demilitarized Zone, and anticipate the Green and Attila Lines of Cyprus. Conran's and Clancy's translation of *ynn* as 'ashtrees' misses the trace of violence which, consciously or not, other translations succeed in evoking with 'ash' or its plural: 'down in the ashes . . . dividing the meadows' (R. S. Thomas).

But despite its commitment to registering the brutality of modern war and the despotism of the modern State, the poem as a whole works hard to *erase* MDLs and DMZs, conceiving of the two fields as a single, unified space – a forcefield in which 'his people' will walk, in the ground of the next stanza, bound together by a current running 'through them, among them, about them' (Clancy). The famous *bwlch* – 'gap, breach' – of the penultimate line is part of the same agenda, as is the poem's title. As already suggested, the field-names mirror each other in such a way as to dissolve the sense that they are immutably separate territories. Stanza four, then, offers a map of a Korea-made-whole, not through military intervention and surprise attacks over the 38th Parallel, but through cooperative work on the same ground (Wales-as-Korea, Korea-as-Wales). 'And on the two fields his people walked' is Conran's straightforward translation of Waldo's *Ac ar y ddau barc fe gerddai ei bobl*; R. S. Thomas remaps the original – 'and his people were abroad in both fields' – with a pun that reminds us of the internationalist vision of 'In Two Fields', its insistence on seeing the local in a global context, and its love of paradox. 'Here' is emphatically 'abroad'; OS SN 126 203 is at once Wales, Korea and Cyprus.

Despite the sense of division overcome in stanza four and the resonance of that phrase from Revelation, *dail pren*, 'leaves of a tree', in the penultimate stanza, the final three verses do not offer a single-layered, bright blueprint for some millenarian 'healing of the nations'. If that were so, the poem would be a fractured poem of two sectors. As it is, those 'tremors of anxiety' continue to be registered, even as a dissenting image of unified ground is projected. Even when it doesn't mean to, the Welsh original troubles translators with reminders of war. Of the end of the third stanza – *Tawel ostegwr helbul hunan*, 'Quiet calmer of the troubled self' (Conran) – Rowan Williams remarks:

> The final line defies a straightforward rendering because we have no English word that will do for *gostegwr*: 'silencer' makes you think of guns, which is exactly what you don't want to be evoking just here.[57]

Williams is right to acknowledge that the context is a positive one in that the subject of the line is the Exiled King. Moreover, *gostegwr* itself has nothing to do with guns, and so Williams opts for 'who with a quiet word/ calms the red storms of self'. However, it is typical of 'In Two Fields' that, in transit over the linguistic border, *gostegwr* briefly has to confront another dark 'counterforce' in the word 'silencer', thrown up by the troubled process of translation. And, of course, there's ground to disagree with Williams: it seems to me that 'guns' is precisely what one would wish to evoke here; 'silencer' would be perfectly in tune with the fraught idiom of a poem that is itself, in all its imaginings, a 'troubled self'. (Gerwyn Wiliams's reference to Waldo and the exiled unifier in his 1994 poem 'Dolenni' ['Links'] is disturbed by the presence of a bullet lodged at the heart of the image: *y cyfannwr mawr ei hun/ yn taenu bwletinau brawdgarwch* – in the poet's own translation, published in the same journal as R. S. Thomas's rendering of 'In Two Fields', 'the great unifier himself/ broadcasts bulletins of brotherhood'.[58])

The image of harvest co-operation in the two fields in stanza four – an activity in which Waldo participated on numerous occasions – encodes its very opposite: military attack. Again, the poem's idiom of dissent resolutely resists the comforts of the kind of pastoral that elides socio-political realities. In the lines *Fel gyda ni'r ychydig pan fyddai'r cyrch picwerchi/ Neu'r tynnu to deir draw ar y weun drom*, the harvest field becomes a theatre of war. *Cyrch* – attack – suggests more than mere agricultural effort. The translations reveal three levels of engagement with the word. Joseph Clancy's 'As it was with the few of us once, in the plying of pitchforks/ Or the tedious tugging of thatch out on the heavy moor' neutralizes *cyrch* into a mere mechanical act, as does Gwyn Jones's 'As it was for us few, when wielding our pitchforks/ Or culling reluctant thatch from the heavy rushland' (though 'culling' might be taken as nicely multivalent). R. S. Thomas's collapsing of the image into a single verb, 'pitchforking', evacuates the disturbance entirely, as does R. Gerallt Jones's 'when we were at it with our pitchforks'. Tony Conran and R. M. Jones choose a stronger verb in their 'forrayed [*sic*] with pitchforks', given that the primary sense of 'foray' is 'a hostile or predatory incursion, a raid'. However, modern usage has diluted that meaning, rendering 'foray' more inoffensive. So it is left to Rowan Williams to suggest the force of Waldo's *cyrch*: 'as it was for some of us, the little group/ who'd been all day mounting assault/ against the harvest with our forks'. ('An attack of pitchforks', Williams notes in his gloss on his translation, would have been too 'abrupt'.) Is there not also an instability of tone in Williams's translation, a hint of playfulness? '[L]ittle group', the informality of the abbreviated 'who'd', the 'forks' that briefly (don't they?) suggest something more domestic than 'pitchforks', and the general sense of disjunction between vocabulary and context all conspire to produce a dislocating effect that adds to the disturbance generated by 'assault'.

The border space between stanzas four and five asks us to cross a boundary of time into a tense, and briefly tenseless, new field: *Yr oedd yr heliwr distaw yn bwrw ei rwyd amdanom.// O, trwy oesoedd y gwaed ar y gwellt a thrwy'r goleuni y galar* – 'The silent hunter was drawing his net about us.// O through the ages of blood on the straw and through the light the lamenting' (Gwyn Jones). Commentators have drawn attention to the echo here of the famous poem in the ninth-century saga cycle, *Canu Heledd*, about the effects of endless war on *Y Dref Wen* – the 'White/ Blessed

Town': *Ar wyneh y gwellt y gwaet* ('On the surface of its grass/ straw, the blood'). 'The use of a phrase from a poem of the Welsh Dark Ages', Ned Thomas comments, 'emphasizes the point that is being made about the long centuries of bloodshed'.[59] What commentators have not noted is the appropriateness of the echo to the ground of 'In Two Fields'. Jenny Rowland reminds us that the subject of *Canu Heledd* is 'border history': 'the events portrayed . . . fit the picture most commonly held concerning the formation of the Welsh border . . . [it is] a reflection of the state of Powys in the ninth century when the region had suffered from severe border warfare and repeated conquest for over half a century'.[60] The geography of the White Town is ambiguous, but it has been taken to be a 'border town' – a settlement in contested marchland harried by frontier depredation.[61] The allusion therefore confirms the border politics and supplements the border disturbances of 'In Two Fields'. There is another contour-line to the allusion here that adds another stratum to the pacifist idiom of dissent. *O, trwy oesoedd y gwaed ar y gwellt a thrwy'r goleuni y galar* might also inscribe an allusion to an essay by Waldo's father, J. Edwal Williams, on the militarism of Imperial Britain, published in 1905 in *Y Piwritan Newydd* ('The New Puritan'), the paper of the Pembrokeshire Baptists:

> Mae y rhyfelgarwyr wedi arfer ymrithio fel gwladgarwyr, *drwy yr oesoedd* maent wedi llwyddo i alw i fyny ddrychiolaeth rhyw fudd cenedlaethol. Ty*well*tir afonydd o *waed* . . . (my emphasis)[62]

> (The lovers of war have made a habit of posing as patriots; throughout the ages they have succeeded in invoking the image of some national advantage. Rivers of blood are spilt . . .)

Waldo's line is a compound ghost; father and son inhabit 'In Two Fields' and speak with one voice.

Mawr oedd cydnaid calonnau wedi eu rhew rhyn – 'Great was the leaping together of hearts after the deadening ice' (R. Gerallt Jones): line 38, and therefore formally the poem's 38th Parallel. Significantly, it is another furrowed line. 'Waldo is the only person, so far as I know', says Ned Thomas, to use the word *cydnaid*.[63] The only poet to use it in modern Welsh literature, perhaps, but Waldo would have been familiar with the word from various pre-modern Welsh texts in which, significantly, its context is almost always military or violent (as in *Y Gododdin*'s *Gwyr a gryssyassant buant gytneit* – 'warriors charged, leaping forward together').[64] A positive image is again rendered ambiguous by traces of age-old aggression; the line evokes an assault as well as what Waldo glossed as 'the joy of the heart released'.[65] Rowan Williams's 'think of the force/ of hearts released, springing together' succeeds in registering something of that darker contour. It is from *rhew rhyn* that the hearts are released – a debilitating 'ice age' (Conran, R. M. Jones and Rowan Williams), a 'cruel freezing' (Gwyn Jones), a 'hard frost' (R. S. Thomas), 'hard ice' (Clancy). *Rhew rhyn*, however, signifies more than emotional incapacity, a locking up of our ability to love. It is an image of disempowerment and paralysis central to Waldo's pacifist, anarchist thinking on the tyranny of the State and its ideological apparatus. As Waldo remarks at the end of that 1956 'extended gloss' on 'In Two Fields', 'Why I Refused to Pay the Income Tax':

> . . . the State's authority over us is becoming monstrous. There is talk of moving twelve million of us to shelter from these islands. This is one of the great Ice Ages – a government's ordinance can freeze us when the time comes.[66]

Rhew rhyn is the Cold War within and between individuals and nations. It is a political 'killing frost' whose operations are also registered, as Judith Thompson has persuasively argued in a bravura new historicist analysis, by Coleridge (a formative influence on Waldo) in his unsettled and unsettling cradle-poem, 'Frost at Midnight', written during a period of State repression in the 1790s: 'The frost performs its secret ministry/ . . . the secret ministry of cold'.[67] In response to this big freeze, Waldo envisages an ideological and imaginative thaw, and we cross the second 38th Parallel into the famous image of 'fountains bursting towards the heavens/ And falling back, their tears like the leaves of a tree' (Clancy). (Translators have offered 'bursting', 'breaking out', 'reaching up', 'crashed up', and 'gushing' for the action of Waldo's fountains (*torri tua'r nefoedd*), where 'shooting up' would have been an interesting choice.) 'Tears' is a printer's error, as Waldo explained in his gloss: "When the poem appeared in *Y Faner, dafnau* ['drops'] had become *dagrau* ['tears']. I thought this enriched the poem, and that the reader would recognize that they were tears of emotional release. I let the word be'.[68] Conscripted into print on 13 June 1956, *dafnau* crosses a typographic border, and Waldo chose to dissent from his own idiom when the poem appeared in *Dail Pren* at the end of 1956, no doubt recognizing that 'tears' was more in tune with the stressed utterance of 'In Two Fields'.

Waldo acknowledged that the most singular line in the whole poem, *A'r nos trwy'r celloedd i'w mawrfrig ymennydd* (Conran: 'And Night through the cells of her wide-branching brain') in the final stanza, carries an allusion to George Meredith's 'Lucifer in Starlight' ('the stars,/ Which are the brain of heaven').[69] One might also suggest an allusion here to two poems by Keats (already a presence in the poem in the phrase *dail pren*, of course, two lines back across the border[70]): 'Ode to Psyche' ('branchèd thoughts, new grown with pleasant pain'), and *The Fall of Hyperion. A Dream* ('I ached to see what things the hollow brain/ Behind enwombèd; what high tragedy/ In the dark secret chambers of her skull/ Was acting').[71] The echo of the latter further boosts the political frequencies of 'In Two Fields'. Dramatizing a post-war universe in which the Titans have been violently overthrown by the Olympians, *The Fall of Hyperion* articulates a 'transcendental cosmopolitics'[72] (Leigh Hunt's phrase) that commented directly on historical change and violence in revolutionary and post-revolutionary Europe. And in the poem's dream-vision portal, Keats sought explicitly to work through the poet's responsibilities in a brutal age: from what position, and in what idiom, he asks, should the poet engage with a world he described elsewhere as 'full of Misery and Heartbreak, Pain, Sickness and oppression'?[73] As we have seen, Waldo in 'In Two Fields' is also concerned to formulate an idiom that does not elide historical realities and to identify the poet's role as a dissenting one.

The poem's political climax is achieved in the final two lines in the image of the Exiled King walking 'through some crisis in history', as Waldo put it in his gloss, to occupy the *bwlch* between the two fields. It is an image of the breaching of all 38th Parallels. While the Korean DMZ has ironically always been thoroughly militarized, the *bwlch* is a true DMZ, a site of entente (a word that appropriately tries to meet itself halfway, a frustrated palindrome), and of positive contravention – a breach space that again hints at the ephemerality of borders. Conran, R. M. Jones and R. S. Thomas offer 'breach' for *bwlch*; Clancy chooses 'gap' and Gwyn Jones the more prosaic 'gap in the hedge'; R. Gerallt Jones's 'void' renders the aperture a vacuum rather than a space replete with possibility. Rowan Williams's freer rendering again succeeds in registering the poem's war ground: 'He will arrive, the outlaw,/ the huntsman, the lost heir making good his claim/ to no man's land'. It is a bold choice: the *bwlch* here is that scarred, contested ground that has come to define the absurdity of fruitless face-offs between entrenched forces – as Williams remarks, 'the frontier, the place of terror between the battling armies'. But it is about to be transformed into a place of *rapprochement* by the presence that debouches into it. Williams's gloss draws attention to the pun in his translation: the gap is also '"no *man's* land", which only the divine huntsman can claim as his own'. Reading the poem politically, one might add that it is also no *one* man's land, and, in tune with Waldo's gender politics, *woman's* land, too.

Embedding a work of imaginative literature in its material culture runs certain risks, one of which is a serious blunting of our capacity sensitively to distinguish a poem from a political tract. New historicist analysis can easily traduce a poem by presenting it as a mere aspect or adjunct of history (witness various bloody-minded readings of Wordsworth's 'Tintern Abbey' – another highly fraught 'borderland' poem). However, scrutinizing the 'cosmopolitics' of 'In Two Fields' and its investment in the concepts of ground and space helps to foreground the subtleties of its literary representation and the multivocality of its idiom of dissent. No doubt, for many readers, 'In Two Fields' will remain primarily a religious or visionary poem. This essay has not sought to contest that reading, but it has sought to inflect it to take account of the fact that Waldo, like Blake, was not a compartmentalizer – for Waldo, a religious poem was always thoroughly political (and vice versa). My discussion – a kind of historicized ordnance (in all senses) survey – has also attempted to highlight the way in which a personal poem can function as public intervention. It is offered as a map of unparalleled ground.

The editor and Damian Walford Davies wish to thank Rowan Williams, Hugo Brunner and The Perpetua Press for permission to include the poem 'Between Two Fields', Rowan Williams's rendering of Waldo Williams's 'Mewn Dau Gae'.

Between Two Fields

These two fields a green sea-shore, the tide spilling
radiance across them, and who knows
where such waters rise? And I'd had years
in a dark land, looking: where did it, where did he
come from then? Only he'd been there
all along. Who though? who
was this marksman loosing off bolts
of sudden light? One and the same the lightning
hunter across the field, the hand to tilt
and spill the sea, who from the vaults
above the bright-voiced whistlers, the keen darting plovers,
brought down on me such quiet, such

Quiet: enough to rouse me. Up to that day
nothing had worked but the hot sun to get me going,
stir up drowsy warm verses: like blossom
on gorse that crackles in the ditches, or
like the army of dozy rushes, dreaming
of clear summer sky. But now: imagination
shakes off the night. Someone is shouting
(who?), Stand up and walk. Dance. Look.
Here is the world entire. And in the middle
of all the words, who is hiding? Like this
is how it was. There on the shores of light
between these fields, under these clouds.

Clouds: big clouds, pilgrims, refugees,
red with the evening sun of a November storm.
Down where the fields divide, and ash and maple

cluster, the wind's sound, the sound of the deep,
is an abyss of silence. So who was it stood
there in the middle of this shameless glory, who
stood holding it all? Of every witness witness,
the memory of every memory, the life
of every life? who with a quiet word
calms the red storms of self, till all
the labours of the whole wide world
fold up into this silence.

And on the silent sea-floor of these fields,
his people stroll. Somewhere between them,
through them, around them, there is a new voice
rising and spilling from its hiding place
to hold them, a new voice, call it the poet's
as it was for some of us, the little group
who'd been all day mounting assault
against the harvest with our forks, dragging
the roof-thatch over the heavy meadow. So near,
we came so near then to each other, the quiet huntsman
spreading his net around us.
Listen! you can
just catch his whistling, hear it?

Whistling, across the centuries of blood
on the grass, and the hard light of pain; whistling
only your heart hears. Who was it then, for God's sake?
mocking our boasts, tracking our every trail and slipping past
all our recruiting sergeants? Don't you know?
says the whistling, Don't you remember?
don't you recognise? it says; until we do.
And then, our ice age over, think of the force
of hearts released, springing together, think
of the fountains breaking out, reaching up
after the sky, and falling back, showers
of falling leaves, waters of autumn.

Think every day, under the sun,
under these clouds, think every night of this,
with every cell of your mind's branching swelling shoots;
but with the quiet, the same quiet, the steady breath,

the steady gaze across the two fields, holding still
the vision: fair fields full of folk;
for it will come, dawn of his longed-for coming,
and what a dawn to long for. He will arrive, the outlaw,
the huntsman, the lost heir making good his claim
to no-man's land, the exiled king
is coming home one day; the rushes sweep aside
to let him through.

Rowan Williams. *From the Welsh of Waldo Williams*

NOTES

[1] Damian Walford Davies (ed.), *Waldo Williams: Rhyddiaith* (Cardiff, 2001), 87. All translations from Welsh texts other than 'In Two Fields' are my own.

[2] Robert Rhys, 'Poetry 1939–70', in Dafydd Johnston (ed.), *A Guide to Welsh Literature, 1900–1996*, (Cardiff, 1998), 99; and Ned Thomas, 'Waldo Williams – In Two Fields', in Hans-Werner Ludwig and Lothar Fietz (eds.), *Poetry in the British Isles: Non-Metropolitan Perspectives* (Cardiff, 1995), 262.

[3] Michael Cronin, 'Global Questions and Local Visions' in Alyce von Rothkirch and Daniel Williams (eds.) *Beyond the Difference: Welsh Literature in Comparative Contexts* (Cardiff, 2004), 197.

[4] Rowan Williams, 'Translating Waldo', forthcoming in Damian Walford Davies and Jason Walford Davies (eds.), *Cof ac Arwydd: Ysgrifau Newydd ar Waldo Williams* (Memory and Sign: New Essays on Waldo Williams), (Cyhoeddiadau Barddas, 2006).

[5] Tony Conran translates the names as 'Flower Meadow Field' and 'Flower Field' in *Poetry Wales*, 2:3 (1966), 12–13 and in *The Penguin Book of Welsh Verse* (Harmondsworth, 1967), 258–60. *Blawd* can certainly mean *blodyn* – 'bloom' – but the owner of the fields, Vernon Beynon, confirms that the reference here is to 'flour'. Conran's 'Flower' is queried by Katie Gramich in *New Welsh Review*, 40 (Spring 1998), 84.

[6] See Gerwyn Williams, *Tir Newydd: Rhai Agweddau ar Lenyddiaeth Gymraeg a'r Ail Ryfel Byd* (Cardiff, 2005), 135.

[7] *Rhyddiaith*, 88.

[8] W. D. Erhart and Philip K. Jason (eds.), *Retrieving Bones: Stories and Poems of the Korean War* (New Brunswick, 1999), xx.

[9] Erhart and Jason (eds.), *Retrieving Bones*, xxii.

[10] As well as the anthology cited in the previous note, which contains a useful introduction, along with biographies and bibliographies, see the special issue of *War, Literature and the Arts*, 9:2 (Fall/ Winter 1997), entitled 'I Remember: Soldier-Poets of the Korean War'.

[11] See, for example, Thomas, 'Waldo Williams – In Two Fields', 253–66; the essays by Bedwyr Lewis Jones and Dafydd Elis Thomas in Robert Rhys (ed.), *Waldo Williams: Cyfres y Meistri 2* (Abertawe, 1981), 149–59 and 160–7; and Tony Bianchi's 'Waldo and Apocalypse', *Planet*, 44 (August 1978), 5–12.

[12] *Rhyddiaith*, 90.

[13] The allusion is identified by Waldo in the 'Notes' to the poem at the end of *Dail Pren*.

[14] See Pennar Davies, 'A'r Brwyn yn Hollti', in Rhys (ed.), *Waldo Williams: Cyfres y Meistri 2*, 188, and Hugh Bevan, 'Barddoniaeth y Cae Agored' in the same volume, 256.

[15] See Thomas, 'Waldo Williams – In Two Fields', 253.

[16] The pun is also suggested in the title of Ned Thomas's 1995 reading of the poem 'from the point of view of comparative cultural criticism': 'Waldo Williams – In Two Fields', 253.

[17] Tony Conran (tr.), *Waldo Williams: The Peacemakers* (Llandysul, 1997), 17.

[18] In 'Why I Refused to Pay the Income Tax', Waldo refers to the moral right to judge the State as 'the necessary anarchism at the heart of republicanism'; *Rhyddiaith*, 317.

[19] Conran (tr.), *The Peacemakers*, 21.

[20] See Rowan Williams, *Remembering Jerusalem* (Oxford, 2001), 50–2, and *The Poems of Rowan Williams* (Oxford, 2002), 91–3.

[21] Ned Thomas has recognized the importance of the wartime context: see *Waldo* (Caernarfon, 1985), 23–7 and 'Waldo Williams – In Two Fields', 262.

[22] Ned Thomas rightly remarks that subsequent conflicts awakened in Waldo 'deep and early levels' of his experience, yielding poems that 'respond to present events', but which at the same time echo the initial experience, investing it with a 'philosophical frame'; see *Waldo*, 24.

[23] See my '"Cymodi â'r Pridd": Wordsworth, Coleridge, a Phasg Gwaredol Waldo Williams' ('"Reconciliation with the Soil": Wordsworth, Coleridge and Waldo Williams' Easter Deliverance'), forthcoming in Damian Walford Davies and Jason Walford Davies (eds.) *Cof ac Arwydd: Ysgrifau Newydd ar Waldo Williams*.

[24] Saunders Lewis's phrase describing 'The Dead Children'; see '*Dail Pren*', in Rhys (ed.), *Waldo Williams: Cyfres y Meistri 2*, 266.

[25] See *Rhyddiaith*, 279–90.

[26] *Rhyddiaith*, 282–3.

[27] See Janet Davies, 'The Fight for Preseli, 1946', *Planet,* 58 (August/September 1986), 3–9.

[28] A point made by Rowan Williams in an interview (2 February 2005) for the BBC Wales *On Show* documentary *Waldo Williams: Peacemaker*, broadcast 24 March 2005. For interesting comments on Waldo and the 'political life . . . of home', see Conran (tr.), *The Peacemakers*, 23.

[29] See *Rhyddiaith*, 83 and 85.

[30] R. Gerallt Jones, in *Poetry of Wales, 1930–1970* (Llandysul, 1974), xxi.

[31] Thomas, 'Waldo Williams – In Two Fields', 264, and Dafydd Elis Thomas, 'Mewn Dau Gae', in Rhys (ed.), *Waldo Williams: Cyfres y Meistri 2*, 166.

[32] *Rhyddiaith*, 307-8, 311.

[33] *Rhyddiaith*, 312. Ned Thomas's translation, published in *Planet*, 37/38 (May 1977), 9–13 under the title 'War and the State', misconstrues the subject of Waldo's sentence at this point, making the United Nations (rather than the US, as Waldo intended) seem the hasty aggressor. This is confirmed by Waldo's formulation in 'Sovereignty and Brotherhood': see *Rhyddiaith*, 307.

[34] Quoted in Anthony Farrar-Hockley, *The British Part in the Korean War: A Distant Obligation* (London, 1990), 113.

[35] See *Rhyddiaith*, 90, 100, 317.

[36] *Rhyddiaith*, 87–9.

[37] *Rhyddiaith*, 84.

[38] Jeffrey Grey, *The Commonwealth Armies and the Korean War* (Manchester, 1988), 22.

[39] Peter Lowe, *The Origins of the Korean War* (London, 1986), 14.

[40] Waldo's censure of the US as manipulative antagonist in the 1956 prose texts is curious. That Korea was in many ways a superpower 'proxy-war' is not in doubt; however, the absence of any mention of North Korean aggression and the role of the USSR is puzzling.

[41] For an account of 'the contortions of British manpower policy' at this time, see Grey, *The Commonwealth Armies and the Korean War*, 36–45 and 193, and Farrar-Hockley, *The British Part in the Korean War: A Distant Obligation*, 111–22. I would like to thank Jeffrey Grey for discussing with me the military compulsion in operation at the time.

[42] Ashley Cunningham-Boothe and Peter Farrar (eds.), *British Forces in the Korean War* (Leamington Spa, 1988), 5. See also Tom Hickman, *The Call-up: A History of National Service* (London, 2004), 75 and 100.

[43] See R. F. Holland, *Britain and the Revolt in Cyprus, 1954–1959* (Oxford, 1998). I am grateful to Robert Holland for information relating to the compulsory dimension of British involvement in Cyprus.

[44] Nicholas Roe, *Wordsworth and Coleridge: The Radical Years* (Oxford, 1988), 272.

[45] Walking up through Weun Parc y Blawd and Parc y Blawd to visit his friend Jack Beynon in Y Cross farm, Waldo would pass a plot of land known as 'Bwlch-y-ddwy-Sir' – 'Two Counties Gap' – on which in 1966 he wrote an *englyn*.

[46] See *Rhyddiaith*, 251.

[47] See http://www.hmso.gov.uk/legislation/wales/wsi2002/20023270e.htm. I am grateful to Vernon Beynon, the owner of the two fields, for information relating to the county boundaries.

[48] See *Rhyddiaith*, 305.

[49] For Conran's translation, see note 5; R. M. Jones (his translation is marked 'tr. R. M. J. on A. Conran'), *Highlights in Welsh Literature: Talks with a Prince* (Swansea, 1969), 119–21; R. Gerallt Jones (ed.), *Poetry of Wales, 1930–1970* (Llandysul, 1974), 219–21; Gwyn Jones (ed.), *The Oxford Book of Welsh Verse in English* (Oxford, 1977), 219–20; Joseph Clancy (tr.), *Twentieth-Century Welsh Poems* (Llandysul, 1982), 135–6; R. S. Thomas, *Modern Poetry in Translation*, new series 7 (Spring 1995), 156–7; and see note 20 for Rowan Williams's translation.

[50] Williams, *Remembering Jerusalem*, 7 and 50–2, and *The Poems of Rowan Williams*, 8.

[51] Williams, 'Translating Waldo'. At the end of his gloss, Williams interestingly gives a sense of translation as conflict: 'It is entirely appropriate to end with an admission of total defeat. Poetic translation is like that. But my aim has been to show that the process of translating is not just a losing battle . . . Waldo's combination of density and luminosity makes him a specially significant partner in the complex engagement of translating'.

[52] Williams, 'Translating Waldo'.

[53] See *Rhyddiaith*, 307 and William Stueck, *The Korean War: An International History* (Princeton, 1995), 361.

[54] Thomas, *Waldo*, 25, and 'Waldo Williams – In Two Fields', 261 and 262.

[55] Gwyn Thomas, 'Mewn Dau Gae', in *Dadansoddi*, 14 (Llandysul, 1984), 59; T. S. Eliot, *Collected Poems, 1909–1962* (London, 1980), 218.

[56] Thomas, *Waldo*, 25.

[57] Williams, 'Translating Waldo'.

[58] See *Modern Poetry in Translation*, new series 7 (Spring 1995), 162 and 164.

[59] Thomas, 'Waldo Williams – In Two Fields', 263.

[60] Jenny Rowland, *Early Welsh Saga Poetry* (Cambridge, 1990), 120.

[61] Gwyn Thomas describes Y Dref Wen as a 'border town' (*tref ffin*) in his analysis of 'In Two Fields', but does not explore the significance of the allusion in the context of Waldo's interest in borders. See Thomas, 'Mewn Dau Gae', 60.

[62] *Y Piwritan Newydd*, Vol. 2, No. 17 (November 1905), 11. See *Rhyddiaith*, 116–17.

[63] Thomas, 'Waldo Williams – In Two Fields', 264.

[64] See A. O. H. Jarman (ed.). *Aneirin: Y Gododdin* (Llandysul, 1988), 24 and

25. For other citations of *cydnaid* and its belligerent contexts (for example, *kynawon owein kyngrein kytneit*; *Aeth pob gwlad yn gad gydnaid*), see the entry in *Geiriadur Prifysgol Cymru*.

[65] See *Rhyddiaith*, 88–9.

[66] *Rhyddiaith*, 318.

[67] I quote the first, 1798, version. See Judith Thompson, 'An Autumnal Blast, A Killing Frost: Coleridge's Poetic Conversation with John Thelwall', *Studies in Romanticism,* 36:3 (Fall 1997), 427–56.

[68] *Rhyddiaith*, 89.

[69] See *Rhyddiaith*, 97; Waldo mistakenly cites Swinburne as the author.

[70] Waldo wrote in a letter of 19 June 1956 to J. Gwyn Griffiths and Kate Bosse-Griffiths: 'As to the book's title, *Dail Pren* is the title I've had in my mind for it for years. Do you remember Keats saying that poetry must come as the tree gives forth its leaves?'; see *Rhyddiaith*, 84 and 345.

[71] John Barnard (ed.), *John Keats: The Complete Poems* (Harmondsworth, 1987), 342 and 442.

[72] Quoted in Nicholas Roe, *John Keats and the Culture of Dissent* (Oxford, 1997), 56. Hunt's comment was on *Hyperion,* the earlier incarnation of *The Fall of Hyperion.*

[73] Hyder E. Rollins (ed.), *The Letters of John Keats, 1814–1821,* 2 vols (Cambridge, 1958), I, 281.

FRAMING WALES: THE PARLIAMENT FOR WALES CAMPAIGN, 1950–1956[1]

Emily Charette

One underlying assumption unites the essays in this collection: discourse matters. The discourse of protest matters because it forcefully challenges status quo values and beliefs thereby opening up new ways of seeing and thinking about the world; through dissent the unimaginable becomes imaginable. But how exactly does this transformation occur? What are the mechanisms by which dissenting discourse feeds into the processes of social and political change? If we are to understand the impact of such discourse, we should ask not only about the message of dissenting individuals and groups, but also about the political and cultural constraints facing them as they seek to construct and convey their message. The case study which follows will adopt an analytical framework from the literature on social movements to examine the opportunities and constraints facing challengers of the status quo as they sought to further the cause of Welsh autonomy through the Parliament for Wales Campaign. By focusing on this episode of dissent, I hope to shed light on the production and impact of dissenting discourse. Before doing so, however, I must briefly discuss the social movement framework that will be used to guide the analysis.

Scholars working on the study of social movements were quite slow to recognize the importance of discourse. Early work in the field focused on movement emergence and, more specifically, on the material resources and organizational networks that made mobilization possible.[2] A second generation of scholars explored the interplay of social movements and the external political environment in which they operated.[3] Not until the mid-1980s, with the publication of David Snow and colleagues' research on 'framing', did discourse become central to social movement research.[4] Framing has been defined as 'the conscious strategic efforts by groups of people to fashion shared understandings of the world and themselves that legitimate and motivate collective action,'[5] and comprises three elements: 'diagnosis' – putting into words what is wrong with society; 'prognosis' – how this wrong should be ameliorated; and 'motivation' – elaboration of the rationale for engaging in collective action.[6] The challenge for movement actors and organizations is to present grievances and demands in a frame that resonates with a wider audience and also successfully copes with the counter-frames of opponents and representatives of the status quo. More recently scholars have adopted the term 'discursive opportunity structure' to designate the pre-existing environment of status quo values and beliefs in which framing occurs and which may facilitate or constrain framing.[7] Synthesizing the vast body of social movement research makes it possible to examine the dissenting discourse of the Parliament for Wales Campaign in the context of internal movement characteristics, external political factors, and status quo values and beliefs, thereby furthering an understanding of *how* the campaign mattered for social and political change in Wales. At the same time, this social movement framework should raise new questions for students of discourse and social change, thus encouraging them to look in new directions as they seek to understand the discourse of dissent.

The Parliament for Wales Campaign

In July 1950 several prominent political, cultural and religious figures from across Wales gathered in Llandrindod to voice their support for Welsh home rule and to launch a petition for a devolved parliament. Thus began the Parliament for Wales Campaign (PWC). The charismatic Labour MP for Merthyr Tydfil, S.O. Davies, and the President of Plaid Cymru, Gwynfor Evans, were among those elected at the conference to serve on the campaign's executive committee. Liberal MP Lady Megan Lloyd George was nominated President. For the next six years the campaign organized speaking tours that crisscrossed Wales to raise public awareness of the campaign's aims and to gather signatures. Finally, on 7 April 1956, Labour MP Goronwy Roberts presented the petition with its 240,000 signatures, representing fourteen per cent of the population of Wales, to Parliament.[8] Elwyn Roberts, secretary of the campaign, felt that the years of effort had 'done a great deal of good' and reflected that 'self-government is most certainly very much nearer now than it was five years ago and people are optimistic, as a result of the work done by the campaign, that a large measure of devolution will be granted to Wales in the near future.'[9] And yet by December of the same year, after failing to receive a government response, Roberts lamented that, 'All the Petition's papers are now in cardboard boxes, one on top of the other, rotting through dampness.'[10] The PWC was defunct, its ultimate goal unrealized. Four decades would pass before Wales would be granted a measure of Home Rule.

The PWC would appear to have been a monumental flop. Historians cite myriad factors that contributed to the campaign's impotence: a lack of financial and human resources; public satisfaction with the Welfare State; the centralizing Labour party's dominance of Welsh politics and society; the general ineffectiveness of petitions as tools for political change; socio-cultural differences that rendered problematic appeals to 'Welsh' identity, etc.[11] At the same time, we are urged not to dismiss the campaign as inconsequential. In addition to a quarter-million mildew-stained signatures, the campaign is credited with bringing considerable attention to the issue of devolution, helping to pave the way for the establishment of the Welsh Office in 1964.[12] Others also point out that the campaign raised the profile of Plaid Cymru and contributed to the party's maturation.[13] But underlying these historical, context-specific facts, what mechanisms and processes were at work? *How* does a challenge to the status quo produce social and political change and what is the nature of that change?

Political and Discursive Opportunities:
A Home Rule Cacophony

Given our tendency to view the Second World War and the rise of the Welfare State as overwhelming forces for the centralization, integration and assimilation of the British state and society, it is easy to forget the undercurrent of pro-devolution sentiment that built up during the war. This minority voice did not disappear in the post-war period, as Labour MPs from north and west Wales added their voices to those from the Liberal Party and industry who insisted Wales was ill-served under the status quo.[14] At the same time, a change in the leadership of Plaid Cymru brought a shift in the party's guiding values and beliefs that enabled the nationalists to see the post-war landscape as ripe with opportunities for promoting institutional change. This convergence of political and discursive opportunities provided the impetus for Wales's first post-war Home Rule campaign.

Although the Labour party had officially supported an elected assembly for Wales since 1918 (a pledge enshrined in Clause IX of the party's constitution), the leadership's ideological allegiance to state centralism ensured that the party did not embrace Home Rule as a campaign issue. Nevertheless, during the Second World War there was increasing pressure from within the party for some measure of devolution. Welsh Labour MP S. O. Davies believed the devastating effects of the Depression might have been mitigated in Wales had there been a Secretary of State to cater for the nation's specific needs.[15] He and the then ardently pro-devolutionist MP James Griffiths further argued that wartime levels of full employment and industrial output would vanish in the postwar period without coordinated recovery planning tailored to fit Wales's unique social and economic make-up.[16] Concessions from the Coalition Cabinet included a Welsh Reconstruction Advisory Committee and, from 1944, an annual 'Welsh Day', when Welsh affairs alone were discussed in the House of Commons; but these did little to satisfy the demands of devolutionists.

In the first general election following the war, nationalistic Labour candidates from north Wales published a broadsheet, *Llais Llafur* ('Labour Voice'), in which they listed their campaign promises for Wales: a Secretary of State; an economic planning authority; a radio corporation; an end to emigration; and a north-south road link. However, the Attlee government was unwilling to appoint a Minister dedicated to Welsh affairs, with Attlee himself writing 'that it would be a mistake to think that Wales could achieve economic well-being altogether apart from considerations of policy for Britain as a whole; nor do I accept the view that the appointment of a Secretary of State would solve the economic problem.'[17] The government instead offered an annual White Paper covering government activities in Wales, so-called 'Quarterly Conferences of Heads of Government Offices in Wales' and, in 1947, a Welsh Regional Council of Labour.[18] On the heels of a Conservative Party pledge of a Cabinet Minister for Wales in 1948, the Labour Cabinet resigned itself to establishing an Advisory Council for Wales and Monmouthshire. Gwyn A. Williams writes that in the period from 1945 to 1948, 'the Labour government seriously applied the idea of social planning and social engineering in the interests of Wales considered as a community',[19] but for devolutionists such as Liberal MP Lady Megan Lloyd George, the government had offered little more than 'half-hearted concessions to Welsh public opinion'.[20] Proponents of change pointed to Scotland, where the work of a proactive Secretary of State, Tom Johnston, had brought concession after concession from the Government during the war, including a Scottish Council of State, a Scottish Council of Industry and a North of Scotland Hydro-Electric Board. In contrast, many argued, the special needs of Wales had been woefully ignored.[21] What is more, government land-grabs for military training facilities and afforestation (which necessitated the displacement of Welsh-speaking communities) were taken as proof of the government's callous disregard for Wales and the Welsh people, leading to a chorus of protest from Labour MPs, Liberals and Communists as well as nationalists.[22]

Coinciding with this rising pressure for devolution was a shift in the beliefs and values of the Plaid Cymru leadership, allowing the party to reach out to sympathetic elites. Under the leadership of Saunders Lewis from 1926 to 1939 the party 'was more of a pressure-group on behalf of the language than an organized political party.'[23] Lewis believed that Welsh language and culture, especially Christianity, were under threat from industrialization and urbanization. Although he believed that 'you cannot artificially encourage the language and literature and arts of a people and at the same time refuse them any economic and political recognition',[24] he devoted little effort to identifying political solutions to what he saw as the death of Welsh culture, while his antipathy towards state-socialism and mass unionism meant he paid scant attention to the economic situation facing the industrial areas of Wales. He wrote in his *Ten Points of Policy* that 'agriculture should be the chief industry of Wales and the basis of its civilization'[25] and envisioned Wales as a society of small-property holders in which large scale capitalism and the working class would disappear. According to Kenneth O. Morgan, the party was therefore seen by 'the mass of the working population, whatever their language, as a small esoteric group of Utopian fanatics'.[26] Furthermore, Lewis was an admirer of Maurice Barrès of the French New Right and an ardent Roman Catholic whose views often came across as illiberal and anti-democratic; something which, in addition to the party's neutral stance when the Second World War broke out, caused detractors to accuse the party of extremist nationalism and fascism.[27]

There were other thinkers within the party, however, who saw the need to address Wales's contemporary economic situation as a means of appealing to an audience beyond the Welsh-speaking intelligentsia. This faction of the party came to the fore with the election of Gwynfor Evans to the party presidency in 1945. Under his guidance, the party developed a more specifically political outlook and undertook serious electioneering for the first time. Much of the impetus for this shift in perspective came from party spokesman D. J. Davies (a former member of the Independent Labour Party). In *The Economics of Welsh Self-Government*[28] and *Can Wales Afford Self-Government?*[29] (the latter written with his wife, the Irish economist Noëlle Davies), Davies presented a detailed analysis of Wales's economic handicaps and elucidated solutions based on cooperative, decentralized socialism such as he had seen at work in Denmark. Additionally, he and his wife helped to clarify the party's constitutional preferences (dominion status) and pushed the party to appeal to the Anglophone community, leading to the 1932 launch of the party's English-language newspaper, the *Welsh Nationalist* (later the *Welsh Nation*). With a 'leftish' vision (albeit anti-statist) and a loosening of its strict Welsh-only policy, the party began to develop goals that chimed with those advocated by devolutionists. Thus the suggestion that Liberals, Communists, and some Labour MPs – all of whom in the late 1940s were calling for some form of Welsh Parliament – might join forces with members of Plaid Cymru in a campaign for a parliament was not entirely beyond the pale. Therefore, although Plaid had begun its own 'Parliament for Wales in Five Years' campaign in 1949, the Plaid leadership met with members of the Liberal party that same year to discuss the possibility of conducting a joint campaign. Because they felt such a campaign was more likely to succeed if it were not affiliated with any single party, they decided that *Undeb Cymru Fydd* (The New Wales Union/Future Wales Union – an apolitical nationalist pressure group promoting Welsh language and culture) should manage the campaign.[30] With no party affiliation, the PWC was able to attract supporters from across the political spectrum. Nationalistic Labour MPs such as Goronwy Roberts (who had previously refused to associate with members of Plaid, a party he associated with 'perverted nationalism'[31]) could now be seen speaking on the same platform as the nationalists, promoting the same cause.[32]

From this overview of the build-up to the launch of the PWC, we can see how nationalists, despite an apparent lack of political opportunities, can take advantage of discursive opportunities and sympathetic elites. The pressure on nationalists to engage with other organizations and politicians can be great, particularly when making initial forays into party politics, because such cooperation exposes a nationalist party to an audience far wider than the devoted nationalists who comprise its natural base. On this new stage, nationalists have the opportunity to put forth the image they desire of themselves, which may help to counteract anti-nationalist rhetoric coming from other quarters, thereby putting to rest public misconceptions about nationalist aims and beliefs. But brokerage of this nature – between nationalists and other political parties – often comes at a heavy cost.

Ideological Constraints: What Key Are We In?

The PWC brought together individuals from an array of parties and other organizations who shared the common goal of a devolved parliament for Wales. However, despite the common thread of small-*n* nationalism uniting the group, elements of the various ideologies represented by members of the PWC were mutually incompatible (e.g. communism/liberalism, state centralism/anti-statism, religious nonconformity/atheism); these had to be suppressed if the campaign were to present a united front. As such, the PWC was largely devoid of what David Westby calls *ideological salience*, that is the 'shared commitment and normative accord that prioritizes movement ideology[33] over competing beliefs, commitments or demands.'[34] This lack of ideological salience lay at the heart of framing and organizational weaknesses that were to plague the campaign.

Framing Failures

From the outset, the lack of ideological salience prevented campaign organizers from effectively framing their demands. First, disagreements about the fundamental causes of Wales's social and economic problems meant the campaign's organizers could not cogently explain to the public why Wales ought to have a devolved parliament (i.e. diagnosis of the problem). Second, the campaigners could not agree on a detailed plan for a future parliament's structure, powers and duties (i.e. prognosis). At the campaign launch it was decided that the formal aim was a parliament with legislative and administrative powers on the Northern Ireland model, but this left plenty of unanswered questions.

The executive were sensitive to criticisms that they had failed to put their proposals into concrete form, and they therefore published a pamphlet in an attempt to clarify their arguments and aims. In *Parliament for Wales* they spoke of the inability of an overburdened Westminster to deal adequately with Welsh affairs. They called for 'self-government within the framework of the United Kingdom' and a 'Parliament with adequate legislative authority in Welsh affairs,' while Westminster would remain in charge of issues of 'wider concern'.[35] As the *Western Mail* of 29 July 1953 rightly commented, the pamphlet came across as 'not so much a plan as a series of statements which at present there is not overmuch effort made to justify.' The weaknesses in the committee's framing are neatly highlighted in a 1954 letter from a campaign opponent.[36] Writing to Elwyn Roberts on why he would not lend his support to the PWC, Caradog Jones, Labour's candidate in Montgomeryshire throughout the 1950s, explained that he found the campaign committee's argument in *Parliament for Wales* too shallow with 'a number of dubious, unsubstantiated and misleading statements of opinion . . . presented as statements of fact.' He criticized the committee for claiming to 'have the solution to the problems before they have established the facts, which will show the nature of the problems.' The committee had failed to undertake much-needed research, a 'thorough objective investigation of the Welsh scene'. More seriously, he accused the committee of playing on emotions such that, 'people in Mid and South Wales expect [a Welsh parliament] to achieve the most startlingly contradictory utopias.' The efforts of the campaign caused him to be 'alarmed at the disappointment, and possibly cynicism, which will follow on the non realisation of wishful thinking by numbers of decent ordinary folk'. Ideologically-ambiguous framing, lacking in empirical evidence, meant that many potentially valuable recruits to the campaign were beyond reach.

Additionally, speaking tours were conducted across Wales in a consciousness-raising effort, and although these raised the profile of the PWC, the dominance of Plaid Cymru members among the campaign's activists and their use of partisan rhetoric led to public confusion about the nature and goals of the campaign. Although he later switched his allegiance to Plaid Cymru, the dominant figure in North Wales Labour politics, Huw T. Edwards, highlighted the problems Plaid dominance was causing the supposedly non-partisan PWC: 'If one looks at the joint campaign meetings, one finds leaders of Plaid attacking the Government right and left, attacking mercilessly leaders of the party who precede or follow its speakers, creating the impression that the campaign is secondary in importance to the success of Plaid Cymru . . . We are not ready to join a campaign to hear Cliff Prothero [Secretary of the Welsh Regional Council of Labour] and other leaders vilified.'[37]

Unable to frame effectively, the campaign was reduced to a fevered drive for signatures. The purpose of the petition was 'to tell the government (and Parliament) that the people of Wales want to govern themselves as befits the citizens of a civilized nation and to show Parliament that the people of Wales can unite together on matters of vital interest',[38] but empirical evidence demonstrating the practical need for a Welsh Parliament was never presented. The driving mentality was 'The more signatures [the petition] gets, the more Wales will get.'[39] Little thought was given to what substantive claims the signatures represented. No one in the campaign seemed to consider that a petition alone could not force the Government to take action, that with no major party wholeheartedly supporting the campaign and/or no threat of sanctions for failure to act, combined with a public confused about campaign aims, there was little force behind a quarter of a million signatures.

Organizational Constraints

We know from the literature on social movements that a lack of financial and human resources does not necessarily spell disaster for a movement.[40] Through framing that creates a clear boundary between movement participants and the target of movement claim-making, in other words by creating a sense of 'us' and 'them', a movement can contribute to group solidarity and a sense of collective identity.[41] This lends the movement an emotional force that may be strong enough to compensate for a lack of financial resources or mass support.[42] In the case of the PWC, however, the lack of ideological salience prevented the cultivation of a sense of 'we-ness' and amplified organizational weakness.

The perceived need to appeal to as wide an audience as possible and to maintain the support of high-profile figures such as Lady Megan circumscribed the tactical choices available to those running the campaign. The desire of the Plaid leadership for the party to be seen as 'reasonable' in order to win elections had the same effect. Therefore, although nationalists provided the core of administrative support for the campaign and Gwynfor Evans was heavily influenced by Gandhi, civil disobedience was never deployed in the name of the PWC; the gathering of signatures on the petition (against the background of the occasional rally or parade) was the limit of the claim-making activities. The lack of ideological salience underlying the campaign and the concomitant impotence of the campaign's framing strategies and tactics meant that the campaign failed to engage both its participants and the public at an emotional level. As a result, few people saw the campaign as a priority. Canvassing was often hampered because volunteers were involved with other campaigns or events.[43] MPs and other community figures who provided the public face of the campaign also had other concerns, as is evident from the frustration of campaign secretary (and Plaid Cymru member) Dafydd Miles in a letter to Noëlle Davies: 'Breconshire is the key to South Wales . . . It has a Labour MP . . . who has really shown more support than any other MP', adding, 'recent parliamentary and extra-parliamentary activity has made it impossible for Mr Tudor Watkins to make the organizational drive which he had intended . . . The petition forms have been in Brecon for months, but . . . the elections cut across everything.'[44]

Furthermore, without effective framing to engage the public, the campaign was unable to attract sufficient donations to cover costs.[45] Area secretaries, who had not been paid for months, were informed that they were expected to raise sufficient sums to cover their own salaries and expenses.[46] Additionally, the inability to appeal to the public through framing meant the campaign was over-reliant on Megan Lloyd George. Lady Megan had strong pulling power, and local committee leaders were clamouring for her services to rally volunteers and support more generally, but she proved unreliable – often failing to keep speaking engagements[47] – and, what is more, expensive, demanding that the campaign provide her with transport to speaking engagements and suitable hotel arrangements when necessary.[48]

In this episode of dissent we have seen that a lack of ideological salience prevented the campaign from surmounting a lack of human and financial resources, and indeed served to compound these weaknesses. From the outset the campaign was unable to attract devoted followers willing to donate their time and money to the cause, and this in turn limited the campaign's capacity to diffuse its message more broadly. The framing and organizational weaknesses that resulted from the campaign's lack of ideological salience left it vulnerable to attack from opponents.

Political and Discursive Constraints: The Labour Machine

The status quo values and beliefs that predominated in Wales at the time of the PWC were largely those espoused by the Labour Party. Particularly in the densely-populated coal-mining areas of the South Wales valleys, the Labour Party had by the 1920s usurped the Liberal values and beliefs of community and egalitarianism that had characterized Wales until the 1920s. Labour came to supremacy by presenting itself as the protector of workers' rights, while the traditional focus of the Liberal Party on issues such as Church Disestablishment, Temperance, and Education no longer reflected the interests of the Welsh working class. As such, the majority of Welsh people came 'to ally with particular [Labour] world views' and then, 'given [their] majoritarian status, effectively appropriated a Welsh identity . . . creating a Welshness in its own image.'[49] From the post-Depression era, these world views were rooted in the Welfare State and state centralism, trade unionism and international class obligations and duties.[50]

This discursive environment into which the PWC was born was structurally reinforced by the hegemony of the Labour machine. Morgan describes the 'solidarity, loyalty and social patriotism' of the Labour movement in Wales during the Second World War, pointing out that this was partly because the movement had become firmly entrenched in the governing process; at the local level, 'Labour's control was total' in much of the industrialized South.[51] Morgan also observes that the post-war economic boom and low unemployment rate (three per cent) were 'due in large measure to the market opportunities temporarily opened up as defeated powers like Germany or Japan strove to rebuild, alongside the assistance of Marshall Aid from America, but Labour claimed the credit for full employment, as well as the Welfare State and "fair shares" and the great majority of Welsh people seemed disposed to agree.'[52] Indeed, Labour consistently polled far ahead of any other party in Wales, even winning 27 out of 36 Welsh seats in the 1951 general election which saw the Conservatives returned to power.

The PWC posed a direct threat to the Labour Party's ideational and structural hegemony in Wales; in arguing the case for a Welsh parliament, the PWC sought to convince the public of the failures of the British State, of the inadequacies of the status quo. The Labour machine lurched into action, using its considerable dominance of political structures and discourse in Wales to limit both the campaign's and – more importantly in the view of the party's Welsh Regional Council – Plaid Cymru's influence over public opinion. The Council was initially dismissive of the campaign, with Council secretary Cliff Prothero portraying it as a 'small number of people who represent no serious body of opinion in Wales'.[53] Indignation increased upon hearing that the PWC launch rally was scheduled for the same day as the All-Labour Rally in Newtown, causing the WRCL officially to 'disassociat[e] itself from the campaign' and call upon 'the whole of the Labour movement in Wales not to send any representatives' to the launch.[54] As the campaign progressed and it became apparent that Labour MPs were playing an important role in it, the WRCL employed various bully-boy tactics in an attempt to control rogue MPs and to limit contact between unions and the campaign.[55] The Council also repeatedly complained to the BBC about the amount of coverage given to the PWC and the relative neglect of Labour-related stories.[56]

This predictable Labour backlash was made all the more effective by the campaign organizers' inability to frame effectively. In failing to clarify the aims, values and beliefs driving the campaign, the Campaign Committee essentially invited the WRCL to do the job for them, thereby ceding 'ownership' of devolution discourse to their opponents. Cliff Prothero was to later describe the campaign as a 'nationalist plot', and the WRCL clearly felt that it was serving Plaid's purposes. [57] Much of the general public was already predisposed to view Plaid in a negative light, despite the change in party attitudes represented by Gwynfor Evans's presidency. Labour Party rhetoric therefore continued in the vein used by Bevan in 1946 to denounce devolution: 'Our nationalist friends are making an enclave, and the vast majority of Welshmen would be denied participation in the government of their own country.' The majority would be 'tyrannized over by a few Welsh-speaking people in Cardiganshire'.[58] The WRCL insisted that the campaign was a 'Trojan horse' for the nationalists who, the public was reminded, remained wedded to economic separation and complete independence from Britain.[59]

As volunteers collected signatures, it is clear that they came up against public confusion and hostility. Having failed effectively to frame their own beliefs and goals, the Executive Committee was forced to define the campaign negatively in response to Labour propaganda and entrenched beliefs. Late in the day, a pamphlet was produced and sent out to all volunteer organizers. *Twenty Questions on the Parliament for Wales Campaign* was designed to aid volunteers who repeatedly found they could not provide straightforward answers to the questions of the general public whose signatures they sought. The pamphlet gives some indication of the type of questions being thrown at hapless volunteers: 'Aren't you really the Welsh Nationalists under another name?'; 'Are you a new political party?'; 'Would everyone in Wales have to learn to speak Welsh?'; 'Would it lead to the splitting up of the TUC?' But rather than elucidating benefits the Welsh might enjoy should they gain a parliament, the document speaks vaguely of 'more direct and therefore more effective consideration of the interests of Wales' and 'acts' that would be 'more suitable to the needs of the people of Wales'.[60] Nowhere are such needs defined.

The WRCL also did what it could to ensure that the public believed the dire consequences in store for its greatest constituency, the miners, should the PWC succeed. When it was announced that a motion in favour of the PWC would be discussed at the South Wales area of the NUM, speaking rights were obtained for Welsh MPs such as James Griffiths (and denied to S. O. Davies) who argued that a Parliament for Wales would lead to a break-up of the NUM (and therefore a loss of bargaining power) and a return to district pay agreements that Welsh miners had previously fought so hard to abolish.[61] The vote resulted in rejection of the Home Rule motion, which campaign secretary Elwyn Roberts viewed as a 'psychological body-blow to the campaign'.[62]

The counter-framing activities of the WRCL were ad hoc and unsophisticated, but nevertheless tapped into deep-rooted values, beliefs, fears and prejudices. They also emphasized the protection of the status quo which, given the economic boom at the time and still-fresh memories of pre-war mass unemployment, many people saw as beneficial. 'Everyone is satisfied with the world the way it is,' observed one campaign supporter, 'and it is hard to make them realize things.'[63] WRCL framing thus resonated with a large body of the public, and proved to have an enduring impact.

Conclusion

The Parliament for Wales Campaign, although unsuccessful, nevertheless had profound consequences. First, it forced the Labour Party finally to define its position on devolution, and in so doing to recognize that Wales had unique problems that were not being properly addressed by the machinery of government. James Griffiths believed 'vagueness' had caused the divisions within the Labour Party in Wales, and Cliff Prothero concurred, writing, 'We must be in a position to tell our people in Wales what we will do when we are returned to power.'[64] As early as 1950 the WRCL was asking 'head office to produce a short pamphlet pinpointing the Government's achievements in Wales',[65] and in 1952 asked members to submit 'a list of problems peculiar to Wales that could be remedied by socialist measures'.[66] Clearly the party thought the campaign was influencing public opinion. The real fear was that Plaid would benefit: 'The Welsh National [*sic*] Party is increasing in numbers . . . because . . . they have a policy – whether it be right or wrong . . . The Welsh National Party say themselves what we want . . . we must have a policy which comes from the Labour party.'[67] Although previously pro-devolutionist, loyal Labour MPs such as James Griffiths had come out firmly against the campaign because it threatened party unity, and this threat forced the party to seek 'a Policy for Wales outside of a Parliament for Wales'. As such, the roots of the 1964 establishment of a Secretary of State of Wales lay in the PWC-fomented arguments and debates over devolution.

The PWC also served to strengthen the ideational divide between an imagined 'North' and 'South' Wales. With Labour allowed to frame the debate in its own terms, an image of an Anglophone, working-class Wales was presented as the true image of the nation. The Welsh-Wales element of the Labour Party could find no voice within the WRCL, and therefore had limited impact on attempts to develop a national policy. The minutes of meetings of the WRCL executive demonstrate that issues of concern to rural constituents, such as transport and language preservation,[68] took a back seat to WRCL attempts to devise ways of industrializing those areas that harboured the strongest nationalist sentiment.[69] Thus, this episode served further to embed pre-existing antipathies between Anglophone and Welsh-speaking communities, and Labour's aversion to policies perceived as singling out Welsh-speaking areas for 'special treatment'. The stage was set, therefore, for later rounds of nationalist claim-making focused on the language and Welsh-speaking communities.

Although scholars disagree about the impact of the campaign on Plaid Cymru,[70] the experience gave the party considerable public exposure and forced the leadership to give serious consideration to ways of appealing to a wider audience. On the other hand, many within Plaid were frustrated with the perceived desertion of principles through co-operating with British parties and supporting a level of devolution that they found unsatisfactory. In addition, many considered the PWC's institutionalized forms of claim-making to be wholly ineffective, sowing the seeds of future divisions within the nationalist movement over means and ends.

Finally, while it is difficult to gauge the impact of the campaign on public attitudes without evidence such as might be garnered from an opinion poll, there is little doubt that the plethora of public meetings and ongoing press coverage raised public awareness. Gwynfor Evans believed that 'the campaign . . . caused many thousands to think about Wales as a nation and awakened in many others the conviction that it should be self-governing';[71] but even those whom the campaign failed to persuade were nevertheless encouraged to think consciously about Welshness and Welsh nationhood. As such, one might say that the Parliament for Wales Campaign opened the door to a new era of politics in Wales: the politics of identity.

NOTES

[1] The author gratefully acknowledges the generous support of the Jean Monet Centre, The Institute of Welsh Politics, and the Department of International Politics at the University of Wales, Aberystwyth.

[2] For a classic example of 'resource mobilization' theory, see John D. McCarthy and Mayer N. Zald, *The Trend of Social Movements in America: Professionalization and Resource Mobilization* (Morristown, NJ, 1973).

[3] Key works examining the so-called 'political opportunity structure' include Doug McAdam, *Political Process and the Development of Black Insurgency, 1930–1970* (Chicago, 1982), and Sidney Tarrow, 'Struggling to Reform: Social Movements and Policy Change During Cycles of Protest,' in *Western Societies Paper 15* (Ithica, NY, 1983).

[4] David A. Snow *et al.*, 'Frame Alignment Processes, Micromobilization, and Movement Participation,' *American Sociological Review*, 51 (1986).

[5] Doug McAdam, 'Conceptual Origins, Current Problems, Future Directions,' in Doug McAdam, John D. McCarthy and Mayer N. Zald (eds.), *Comparative Perspectives on Social Movements* (Cambridge, 1996).

[6] Robert D. Benford and David A. Snow, 'Framing Processes and Social Movements: An Overview and Assessment,' *Annual Review of Sociology*, 26 (2000).

[7] The concept is most fully elaborated in Myra Marx Ferree *et al.* (eds.), *Shaping Abortion Discourse: Democracy and the Public Sphere in Germany and the United States, Communication, Society and Politics* (Cambridge, 2002).

[8] *Western Mail*, 19 April 1956.

[9] NLW, Elwyn Roberts papers, file 30, personal notes 4 June 1956.

[10] J. Graham Jones, 'The Parliament for Wales Campaign, 1950–1956,' *Welsh History Review*, 16, no. 2 (1992), 234.

[11] Robert Griffiths, *S.O. Davies – a Socialist Faith* (Llandysul, 1983), Ch. 7, Jones, 'The Parliament for Wales Campaign, 1950–1956', Elwyn Roberts, 'Ymgyrch Senedd I Gymru,' in John Davies (ed.), *Cymru'n Deffro* (Talybont, 1981).

[12] See, for example, Jones, 'The Parliament for Wales Campaign, 1950–1956', 233.

[13] Gwynfor Evans, *Fighting for Wales* (Talybont, 1997), 191, Laura McAllister, *Plaid Cymru: The Emergence of a Political Party* (Bridgend, 2001), 100.

[14] Kenneth O. Morgan, 'Power and Glory: War and Reconstruction, 1939–1945', in Duncan Tanner, Chris Williams, and Deian Hopkin (eds.), *The Labour Party in Wales, 1900–2000* (Cardiff, 2000), 169.

[15] Jones, 'The Parliament for Wales Campaign, 1950–1956,' 221.

[16] Griffiths, *S.O. Davies – a Socialist Faith*, 163–4.

[17] Quoted in Morgan, 'Power and Glory: War and Reconstruction, 1939–1945', 179.

[18] See J. Graham Jones, 'The Attitude of Political Parties Towards the Welsh Language,' in Geraint Jenkins and Mari A. Williams (eds.), *'Let's Do Our Best for the Ancient Tongue': The Welsh Language in the Twentieth Century* (Cardiff, 2000), 208. Morgan Phillips, general secretary of the Labour Party and a native Welsh speaker, insisted on the 'regional' qualification. See Morgan, 'Power and Glory: War and Reconstruction, 1939–1945,' 178.

[19] G A Williams, *When Was Wales?* (Harmondsworth, 1985), 234.

[20] Quoted in Jones, 'The Parliament for Wales Campaign, 1950–1956,' 209.

[21] Morgan, 'Power and Glory: War and Reconstruction, 1939–1945,' 179–80.

[22] Griffiths, *S.O. Davies – a Socialist Faith*, 51–2.

[23] Kenneth O. Morgan, *Rebirth of a Nation: A History of Modern Wales* (Oxford, 1998), 207.

[24] Quoted in Alan Butt Philip, *The Welsh Question* (Cardiff, 1975), 17.

[25] Quoted in McAllister, *Plaid Cymru: The Emergence of a Political Party*, 53.

[26] Morgan, *Rebirth of a Nation: A History of Modern Wales*, 256.

[27] Accusations that, to some extent, persist today.

[28] D.J. Davies, *The Economics of Welsh Self-Government* (Cardiff, 1931).

[29] D.J. Davies and Noëlle Davies, *Can Wales Afford Self-Government?* 2nd ed. (Cardiff, 1947).

[30] Roberts, 'Ymgyrch Senedd i Gymru,' 96. Several prominent members of Plaid, including Gwynfor Evans, were on the *Undeb*'s council.

[31] A term he used in a 1946 Parliamentary debate, in which he called for a Secretary of State for Wales. See Jones, 'The Attitude of Political Parties Towards the Welsh Language,' 252.

[32] Five Labour MPs supported the campaign: Tudor Watkins (Brecon and Radnor), Goronwy Roberts (Caernarfon), Cledwyn Hughes (Anglesey), T. W. Jones (Merioneth), and S. O. Davies. All but Davies were elected after the war and were the first Labour MPs elected to rural or semi-rural seats. See R. Merfyn Jones and Ioan Rhys Jones, 'Labour and the Nation,' in Duncan Tanner, Chris Williams, and Deian Hopkin (eds.), *The Labour Party in Wales* (Cardiff, 2000), 252.

[33] Movement ideology may be understood as comprising a theory about society (systems or sets of beliefs that explain how social arrangements came to be and how they might be changed or strengthened) linked to a cluster of values about what is right and wrong as well as norms about what to do. See Hank Johnston and Pamela Oliver, 'What a Good Idea! Ideologies and Frames in Social Movement Research,' *Mobilization*, 4, no. 1 (2000), 45.

[34] David L. Westby, 'Strategic Imperative, Ideology and Frame,' *Mobilization*, 7, no. 3 (2002), 291.

[35] Parliament for Wales Campaign, *Parliament for Wales* (1953).

[36] NLW, Caradog Jones papers, file 2, Caradog Jones to Elwyn Roberts, 1 February 1954.

[37] *Liverpool Daily Post*, 24 October 1951.

[38] NLW, Elwyn Roberts papers, file 30, *Twenty Questions on the Parliament for Wales Campaign* (undated pamphlet).

[39] NLW, Noëlle Davies papers, file 23, D. J. Davies speech to Abergavenny Cymreigyddion, 13 March 1952. We see this attitude again when, in 1955, it appeared that a Royal Commission on Welsh Affairs might be appointed along the lines of the Cott Commission on Scottish Affairs, and the executive committee surmised it might be called upon to present evidence. In a letter to local secretaries they wrote, 'the most reliable and conclusive evidence would be an impressive total of signatures to the petition.' See NLW, Elwyn Roberts papers, file 30, PWC executive committee to local secretaries, 30 March 1955.

[40] Doug McAdam, Sidney Tarrow, and Charles Tilly, *Dynamics of Contention* (Cambridge, 2001), 44.

[41] Donatella Della Porta, 'Protest, Protesters, and Protest Policing: Public Discourses in Italy and Germany from the 1960s to the 1980s,' in Marco G. Giugni, Doug McAdam, and Charles Tilly (eds.), *How Social Movements Matter* (Minneapolis, 1999).

[42] Nancy Whittier, 'Meaning and Structure in Social Movements,' in David S. Meyer, Nancy Whittier and Belinda Robnett (eds.), *Social Movements: Identity, Culture and the State* (New York, 2002).

[43] On canvassing problems due to competition from other campaigns and events see NLW, Elwyn Roberts papers, file 31, Minutes of West Wales Area Meeting, 2 July 1954 and NLW, Noëlle Davies papers, file 23, Mary J. Brookes to Noëlle Davies, 18 July 1952.

[44] NLW, Noëlle Davies papers, file 20, Dafydd Miles to Noëlle Davies, 10 March 1952.

[45] For example, a December 1954 fundraising dinner with Megan Lloyd George, which had been expected to erase the campaign's debt of nearly a thousand pounds, managed to raise a paltry forty. See NLW, Elwyn Roberts papers, file 32, Elwyn Roberts to Eiryth Davies, 9 December 1954.

[46] NLW, Elwyn Roberts papers, file 32, Elwyn Roberts to Eiryth Davies and Cliff Bere, 30 November 1954. The two area secretaries eventually resigned, but at the insistence of Lady Megan local secretaries were to be told, 'because of the financial situation we shall have to revert to one organizer for the whole of Wales.' See NLW, Elwyn Roberts papers, file 32, Elwyn Roberts to Eiryth Davies, 8 March 1955.

[47] Writing to Eiryth Davies about an appearance by Lady Megan on 1 July 1954, campaign secretary Elwyn Roberts advised her 'not to make any promises because you are bound to be let down by Lady Megan as I have been dozens of times.' See NLW file 32.

[48] NLW, Elwyn Roberts papers, file 32, Elwyn Roberts to Eiryth Davies, 10 November 1954.

[49] R. Merfyn Jones, 'Beyond Identity? The Reconstruction of the Welsh,' *The Journal of British Studies,* 31, no. 4 (1992), 342.

[50] Jones, 'The Parliament for Wales Campaign, 1950–1956,' 341. While in reality the Labour NEC and Welsh Labour party leadership were much more concerned with 'practical socialism' than with promoting the cause of socialism worldwide (as Labour's failure to support the Republic cause in Spain demonstrated), the radicalism of communists and others in Wales was already being incorporated into Welsh Labour identity. See Robert Stradling, *Wales and the Spanish Civil War: The Dragon's Dearest Cause* (Cardiff, 2004).

[51] Morgan, 'Power and Glory: War and Reconstruction, 1939–1945,' 167, 76.

[52] *Ibid.*, 178.

[53] Quoted in Jones, 'The Parliament for Wales Campaign, 1950–1956,' 212.

[54] NLW, Labour Party (Wales) archives, WRCL executive committee minutes, 26 June 1950.

[55] For example, when a local branch of the National Union of Miners expressed a desire to hold a debate between representative of the PWC and a speaker from the WRCL, Cliff Prothero wrote to them, 'It would be fundamentally wrong for us to have to debate recommendations of our committee along with a member of another political party, particularly when it is borne in mind that the other political party puts up candidates . . . in opposition to Labour candidates'. He

closed by reminding then that the 'South West area of the NUM and its local lodges are affiliated with the WRCL'. See NLW, Labour Party (Wales) archives, WRCL executive committee minutes, 26 April 1954.

[56] For example, Cliff Prothero wrote to the BBC to express the WRCL's 'grave dissatisfaction with the general attitude adopted by the BBC news department' after the BBC sent a van to record the PWC launch while the Labour Party rally on the same day was deemed worthy of no more than a single reporter. See NLW, Labour Party (Wales) archives, WRCL executive committee minutes, 22 June 1950. He also complained of the 'great deal of attention given to a Welsh Nationalist Demonstration in Cardiff'. This was in fact a PWC rally, albeit sponsored by Plaid. See NLW, Labour Party (Wales) archives, WRCL executive committee minutes, 1953.

[57] See Cliff Prothero, *Recount* (Ormskirk, Lancs. and Northridge, CA: GW & A Hesketh, 1982), 68. This view was reinforced when Plaid members were found to have been canvassing for an election while also collecting petition signatures in a Labour stronghold. See NLW, Labour Party (Wales) archives, WRCL executive committee minutes, 25 October 1954.

[58] Quoted in Jones, 'The Attitude of Political Parties Towards the Welsh Language,' 258.

[59] NLW, Labour Party (Wales) archives, WRCL press statement, 27 October 1954.

[60] NLW, Elwyn Roberts papers, file 30.

[61] Jones, 'The Parliament for Wales Campaign, 1950–1956,' 221.

[62] NLW, Elwyn Roberts papers, file 30, PWC executive committee minutes, 18 December 1954.

[63] Quoted in Jones, 'The Parliament for Wales Campaign, 1950-1956,' 226.

[64] NLW Labour Party (Wales) archives, File 28, correspondence of Cliff Prothero and James Griffiths, 24 and 26 January, 1954.

[65] NLW Labour Party (Wales) archives, WRCL executive committee minutes, 5 June 1950.

[66] NLW Labour Party (Wales) archives, WRCL executive committee minutes, 22 September 1952.

[67] NLW, Labour Party (Wales) archives, WRCL Welsh sub-committee meeting minutes, 13 September 1952.

[68] Language was seen to be 'the least difficult of problems . . . there is no cultural tyranny.' NLW, Labour Party (Wales) archives, file 28, Dai J. Davies to Cliff Prothero, 8 October 1952.

[69] See, for example, NLW Labour Party (Wales) archives, Confidential Memorandum on Rural Development in Wales, 16 September 1955.

[70] For example, Philip writes, 'The *Blaid's* involvement in the campaign did the party nothing but good, as its greatly improved showing in the 1955 general election demonstrated.' See Philip, *The Welsh Question*, 261. Davies, on the other hand, sees the campaign as a distraction responsible for 'loss of direction.' See Charlotte Aull Davies, *Welsh Nationalism in the Twentieth Century: The Ethnic Option and the Modern State* (New York, 1989).

[71] *For the Sake of Wales: The Memoirs of Gwynfor Evans.*

BIBLIOGRAPHY

Benford, Robert D., and David A. Snow. 'Framing Processes and Social Movements: An Overview and Assessment'. *Annual Review of Sociology* 26 (2000): 611–39.

Davies, Charlotte Aull. *Welsh Nationalism in the Twentieth Century: The Ethnic Option and the Modern State*. New York: Praeger Publishers, 1989.

Davies, D.J. *The Economics of Welsh Self-Government*. Cardiff: Plaid Cymru, 1931.

Davies, D.J., and Noëlle Davies. *Can Wales Afford Self-Government?* 2nd ed. Cardiff: Plaid Cymru, 1947.

Della Porta, Donatella. 'Protest, Protesters, and Protest Policing: Public Discourses in Italy and Germany from the 1960s to the 1980s'. In *How Social Movements Matter*, edited by Marco G. Giugni, Doug McAdam and Charles Tilly. Minneapolis: University of Minnesota, 1999.

Evans, Gwynfor. *Fighting for Wales*. Talybont: Y Lolfa Cyf., 1997.

Idem., *For the Sake of Wales: The Memoirs of Gwynfor Evans*. Translated by Meic Stephens. 2nd ed. Cardiff: Welsh Academic Press, 2001.

Ferree, Myra Marx, William A. Gamson, Jürgen Gerhards, and Dieter Rucht, eds. *Shaping Abortion Discourse: Democracy and the Public Sphere in Germany and the United States, Communication, Society and Politics*. Cambridge: Cambridge University Press, 2002.

Griffiths, Robert. *S.O. Davies – a Socialist Faith*. Llandysul: Gomer Press, 1983.

Johnston, Hank, and Pamela Oliver. 'What a Good Idea! Ideologies and Frames in Social Movement Research'. *Mobilization* 4, no. 1 (2000): 37–54.

Jones, J. Graham. 'The Attitude of Political Parties Towards the Welsh Language'. In *'Let's Do Our Best for the Ancient Tongue': The Welsh Language in the Twentieth Century*, edited by Geraint H. Jenkins and Mari A. Williams, 249–76. Cardiff: University of Wales Press, 2000.

Idem., 'The Parliament for Wales Campaign, 1950-1956.' *Welsh History Review* 16, no. 2 (1992): 207–36.

Jones, R. Merfyn. 'Beyond Identity? The Reconstruction of the Welsh'. *The Journal of British Studies* 31, no. 4 (1992): 330–57.

Jones, R. Merfyn, and Ioan Rhys Jones. 'Labour and the Nation'. In *The Labour Party in Wales*, edited by Duncan Tanner, Chris Williams and Deian Hopkin, 241–63. Cardiff: University of Wales Press, 2000.

McAdam, Doug. 'Conceptual Origins, Current Problems, Future Directions'. In *Comparative Perspectives on Social Movements*, edited by Doug McAdam, John D. McCarthy and Mayer N. Zald. Cambridge: Cambridge University Press, 1996b.

Idem., *Political Process and the Development of Black Insurgency, 1930–1970*. Chicago: University of Chicago Press, 1982.

McAdam, Doug, Sidney Tarrow, and Charles Tilly. *Dynamics of Contention*. Cambridge: Cambridge University Press, 2001.

McAllister, Laura. *Plaid Cymru: The Emergence of a Political Party*. Bridgend: Seren, 2001.

McCarthy, John D., and Mayer N. Zald. *The Trend of Social Movements in America: Professionalization and Resource Mobilization*. Morristown, NJ: General Learning Press, 1973.

Morgan, Kenneth O. 'Power and Glory: War and Reconstruction, 1939–1945'. In

The Labour Party in Wales, 1900–2000, edited by Duncan Tanner, Chris Williams and Deian Hopkin, 166–88. Cardiff: University of Wales Press, 2000.

Idem., *Rebirth of a Nation: A History of Modern Wales*. Oxford: Oxford University Press, 1998.

Parliament for Wales Campaign. 'Parliament for Wales' (1953).

Philip, Alan Butt. *The Welsh Question*. Cardiff: University of Wales Press, 1975.

Prothero, Cliff. *Recount*. Ormskirk, Lancs. and Northridge, CA: GW & A Hesketh, 1982.

Roberts, Elwyn. 'Ymgyrch Senedd I Gymru'. In *Cymru'n Deffro*, edited by John Davies, 93–120. Talybont: Y Lolfa, 1981.

Snow, David A., Robert D. Benford, E.B. Rochford, and S. Wordes. 'Frame Alignment Processes, Micromobilization, and Movement Participation'. *American Sociological Review* 51 (1986): 464–81.

Stradling, Robert. *Wales and the Spanish Civil War: The Dragon's Dearest Cause*. Cardiff: University of Wales Press, 2004.

Tarrow, Sidney. 'Struggling to Reform: Social Movements and Policy Change During Cycles of Protest'. In *Western Societies Paper 15*. Ithica, NY: Cornell University, 1983.

Westby, David L. 'Strategic Imperative, Ideology and Frame'. *Mobilization* 7, no. 3 (2002): 287–304.

Whittier, Nancy. 'Meaning and Structure in Social Movements'. In *Social Movements: Identity, Culture and the State*, edited by David S. Meyer, Nancy Whittier and Belinda Robnett. New York: Oxford University Press, 2002.

Williams, G.A. *When Was Wales?* Harmondsworth: Penguin, 1985.

GREENHAM AND ITS LEGACY – THE WOMEN'S PEACE MOVEMENT IN WALES IN THE 1980s

Avril Rolph

'A march will be taking place from Cardiff to Greenham Common . . .' These words, which appeared in places as diverse as women's and peace movement newsletters, *The Guardian* and other newspapers, through to *Cosmopolitan*, were the catalyst for what became the major symbol of the women's peace movement in the second half of twentieth-century Britain – the Greenham Common Women's Peace Camp. When the march left Cardiff on 27 August 1981, it was with the intention of drawing attention to the nuclear threat then facing Britain. The press largely ignored it so four women, all from Wales, chained themselves to the fence and the camp followed.

There is little doubt that it was important. What was envisaged as a rally at the gates of the US Base to follow the march turned into an iconic statement of women's refusal to accept nuclear weapons. It remained there for a further 19 years, until finally disbanding in 2000. It received international attention, was the forerunner of several other women's peace camps worldwide, including Seneca Falls, New York; Comiso, Italy; Pine Gap, Australia and, much nearer home, Brawdy in Pembrokeshire, and attracted both enthusiastic support and admiration and vitriolic abuse. As Alison Young noted, 'the women were alternately ridiculed, revered, castigated, humiliated and reviled. In later years they were simply ignored . . .'

Greenham was undoubtedly the catalyst in focusing energy and enthusiasm on the women's peace movement, and prompted many other actions, a number of them in Wales.

A number of writers, particularly Jill Liddington (Liddington, 1998), have made clear that the women's peace movement did not spontaneously re-invent itself after years of inaction once Greenham happened, and there had been a long tradition of women and non-violent activism in Britain, which was largely forgotten by the time Greenham became news. The Women's International League for Peace and Freedom (WILPF), one of the major women's peace organisations, was formed in 1915 following a remarkable meeting of women from many different nations held in The Hague in 1915. In its first annual report it stressed the need to link the Women's Movement and the Peace Movement. In her history of women in Wales in the twentieth century, Deirdre Beddoe quotes evidence that there was a branch of WILPF in Cardiff from 1915–17 (Beddoe, 2000). By the time of the Greenham march, there were still active (if small) branches in Cardiff and Newport, which offered help and support.

However, the peace movement, including the women's peace movement, was at a very low ebb by the end of the 1960s, having lost much of the momentum of the days of the Aldermaston marches of 1958–64. By the late 1960s, anti-Vietnam protests, homosexual and abortion law reform, and the beginnings of the Women's Liberation Movement, which had other priorities than peace, had diverted attention from the peace movement.

It was not until the late 1970s, following the NATO decision of December 1979 to site Cruise and Pershing II missiles in Europe, including Britain, that the threat of nuclear war began to revitalise the peace movement. Women's peace groups, Women Oppose the Nuclear Threat (WONT) began forming in many European countries, including Britain, though not yet in Wales.

One of the major debates provoked by Greenham, and the women's peace actions which followed, was the role played by feminism. The connections and contradictions between feminism and the women's peace movement have been debated in some detail[1] and I do not intend to repeat the debates in this chapter, which is primarily intended to focus on the role of women in the peace movement in Wales in the 1980s.

What is unquestionable is that Greenham was closely connected with 1970s feminism. Sasha Roseneil, in her in-depth sociological study of Greenham Common, suggested that it emerged at a point when the Women's Liberation Movement (WLM) had become large and diverse and had to some extent 'run out of steam'. But it was the 'social networks, political spaces and ideas of the WLM which made Greenham Common possible' (Roseneil, 2000, 32–33).

One of the undoubted strengths of Greenham was the way it attracted women of all kinds, from those who were largely apolitical to radical lesbian feminists, who almost all found a place for themselves there. As Margaretta Jolly explains:

> Associated both with apolitical mothers, fearful for their children's lives, and with radical feminism, the campaign also drew on a less obvious heritage of liberal feminism that was . . . important to the camp's later success. Drawing in thousands more women than nearly any other feminist campaign in Britain at the time, it unexpectedly answered some of the needs of 70s feminists as well as providing a way into feminism for many others, eventually being far more radical than its original design. (Jolly, 2003, 173)

It is certainly apparent from the Wales women's movement newsletters of the period that the networks developed through the WLM which led, for example, to the formation of Swansea and Cardiff Women's Centres, gave considerable strength to initiatives such as action at the Royal Ordnance Factory, Llanishen, the march and peace camps at Brawdy, Greenham support and local events.

The WFLOE Cardiff to Greenham Common March

There have been a number of accounts of the rationale for this march. It is usually credited to Ann Pettitt, an English woman then living in a smallholding near Carmarthen with her partner, Barry Wade, and two small children. Like many people in Wales at that time, they had moved from London in search of a better lifestyle for themselves and their children.

An article written by Ann Pettitt to publicize the forthcoming march and other peace movements in Wales appeared in July 1981 in the Welsh 'alternative' magazine *Arcade: Wales Fortnightly*.

She described how she had become involved in Carmarthen CND, where the members were mainly recent English immigrants like herself. She got to know other women interested in peace issues, and they were inspired by the idea of a women's peace march after reading in Peace News about the Paris to Copenhagen walk organized by Scandinavian Women for Peace. They based the idea of the Greenham march on the same premise, of its being women-led but with men welcome as supporters.

She addresses the criticism that English people living in Wales should be campaigning as energetically for the Welsh language as they were for peace:

> I think we have now to make room in all our lives for both these kind of activities . . . we need those people who, whether Welsh speaking or not, are respected figures in their communities and who sympathise with the aims of the disarmament movement to become active campaigners themselves. (Pettitt, 1981)

In fact, many of the women who became involved in Greenham and other peace activities were Welsh-speaking, including women involved in Plaid Cymru Women's Group.

The march was publicized through press releases to national media, 'alternative' and conventional magazines such as *Cosmopolitan*, and by utilising networks built up by the peace movement, and especially by the Women's Liberation Movement.

Greenham Common United States Air Force base was chosen as the destination of the march as result of the NATO decision of 12 December 1979 to site 96 cruise missiles there. The march also visited other military establishments – the Royal Ordnance Factory at Llanishen in Cardiff (which would later become the site of more peace protests, see below), Caerwent, site of a US Army munitions dump, and Welford RAF weapons store.

Ann Pettitt and other women involved in organising the march decided at an early stage that it would be called The Women for Life on Earth (WFLOE) march, a variation on the American women's peace group, Women and Life on Earth (WALOE) which had been responsible for actions such as the Women's Pentagon Action, which utilized imaginative street theatre and the symbol of the web, which would later become important aspects of Greenham.

The *Wales Women's Directory* for 1984 described WFLOE as

> A network promoting the links between feminism, peace and ecology through the means of non-violent direct action, public education and information exchange. (*Wales Women's Directory*, 1984, 55)

The intention was for the march to include all interested women, not necessarily those in the women's movement, but who, in Ann Pettitt's words, were 'worried, anxious and isolated like myself.' (Pettitt, 1981). She had had a somewhat controversial relationship with feminism, particularly with what she perceived as separatism. Her article on this, 'Feminism for her own good' (Pettitt, 1980), was refused by the women's movement journal *Spare Rib*, many of the collective feeling that it was anti-lesbian. It was eventually published in *Wires*, the national women's liberation newsletter in November 1980.

I interviewed Margery Lewis in 1997 as part of the Feminist History and Archive Project based at the University of Glamorgan. In 1981, she was 65 and a long-time peace campaigner, and became involved at an early stage once she was reassured that it was neither a specifically feminist nor religious march. The oldest walker, then in her 70s, was Effie Leah from near Cardigan, who said of herself, 'I've been on the alternative side of things – we grow tomatoes and shrubs for a market garden. I heard about the march from a stallholder at a medieval fair.' When they arrived at Greenham she, with Eunice Stallard, a grandmother from the Swansea Valley, was one of the first to be chained to the railings.

In all, 40 women, four men and a few children walked all the way, with others dropping in and out along the route. They were a very diverse group, a large proportion of them from Wales, and included Thalia Campbell who made the banners for the march (and continues to make superb banners), and midwife and mother of five children, Helen John, from Llanwrtyd Wells, who would later become a major figure in the camp, and who stood as a WFLOE candidate against James Callaghan in the 1983 General Election.[2] Like many other women who became involved in

feminism and in peace actions, her marriage did not survive once
she became fully committed to Greenham; The *Daily Express* of 8
January 1983, who with the *Daily Mail* and the *Sun*, were always
ready to belittle and sneer at the peace camp, reported her
husband's view that 'she had changed from a housewife and
mother we knew into a fervent feminist and nuclear protestor, it
was very frightening.'

Papers in the WFLOE collection in Glamorgan Records Office
include personal accounts of women taking part; for many it was
the first time they had engaged in a public protest, for others the
first time they had left their children (a few took them along); but
the experience was clearly life-changing for many of them.

Greenham Common Women's Peace Camp

One of the most useful books for giving an impression of the
peace camp in its early years is *Greenham Common: Women at the
Wire*, edited by two women who had been involved in Greenham
themselves, and which quotes extensively from other 'Greenham
women' (Harford 1984). When the rest of the marchers arrived at
the gates of the USAF base, they handed a letter to the base
commander protesting at the arms race and expressing their fears
for the future of their children, and for the world. He dismissively
suggested that they could stay as long as they liked. Presumably
neither he nor they little dreamed how long that would be!

For the next few days there was a succession of women who
chained themselves to the fence, and supplies and messages of
support started to arrive. By the end of the first week they decided
to establish a permanent picket and call it a women's peace camp.
Their aim was to force the government to allow a public televised
debate with the then Defence Secretary, Michael Heseltine, since
the purpose of the march was to draw public attention to the
dangers posed by nuclear weapons.

Media attention was still very limited at the start of the camp, as
it had been throughout the march.[3] The Welsh journal, *Arcade*,
however, published a two-page article in November which was
supportive of the camp, though misleading about the role of men:

They didn't mean to stay . . . It started off as just another march against the Bomb, the only difference being that it was led by women. Now it is turning into an exceptional demonstration and the longer it goes on, the more chance it has of capturing the attention of the media, public opinion and, eventually, the government.

Unfortunately, the author, John Osmond, seemed unwilling to accept the 'men as supporters' rationale, claiming (probably incorrectly) that there were almost as many men as women present, and quotations were given by two of them to balance the two from women, Helen John and Caroline Taylor 'a girl [*sic*] in her late twenties'. The accompanying photograph also featured men in prominent positions around the camp fire. The article also reported that Liney Seward and Caroline Taylor, from near Llandysul, were about to join a women's peace demonstration in Washington, indicating that international links with other women's peace movements had already been established.

The first eviction notices were served in January 1982, followed in May by the first court case held in Newbury Magistrates' Court. This set the pattern for the many court cases that followed – accused women offered to swear the oath by the Goddess, or their children but not God, they sang their evidence, hummed, challenged charges of 'breaching the peace' by pointing out that they were at Greenham Common with the intention of bringing about peace. The defendants at this trial included Helen John, Susan Lamb, Christine King and Thalia Campbell from Wales; four women were imprisoned for refusing to be bound over to keep the peace.

The camp moved firmly into the international spotlight in December 1982, when a massive publicity campaign by women involved in the women's peace movement, attracted 30,000 women from across Britain and beyond to 'Embrace the Base'. The nine-mile perimeter fence was surrounded, and women decorated it with photographs, drawings and other objects.

For the first time massive publicity resulted, with most of the newspapers laying great stress on 'ordinary women' and focusing on the photographs of children and grandchildren, baby clothes and toys tied to the fence as symbols of maternal concern. This was reported in tones varying from admiration that these 'ordinary women' were trying to make a difference, to patronising contempt, depending on the source. The reality of the demonstration was rather different, with a huge variety of women taking part and an extraordinary mixture of objects being fixed to the fence, creating a symbolic barrier of caring, humour, irony and creativity surrounding the threat perceived to lie within the fence.

The following day, 13 December, two thousand women took part in a non-violent demonstration by lying down in the road in front of the entrance gates to prevent traffic entering and leaving the base, returning again and again as they were moved, often quite roughly, by police.

Sîan Evans, who was an active member of Plaid Cymru, was one of the many Welsh women involved in Greenham. She wrote of the 'Embrace the Base' action:

> I was particularly struck by the number of women from Wales at Greenham that day, thousands rather than hundreds, coaches from every corner of Wales. As we approached Gate 4 (referred to as the Welsh gate by the press and everyone else) [we heard] Welsh voices singing 'We shall overcome'. The first hours were more like an Eisteddfod than a political protest – greeting old friends as the Plaid Cymru Women's Section's banner attracted a host of women new to us . . . (Evans, 1983)

Another indication of the support for the action for women across Wales were accounts in local newspapers such as that in the *Cardigan and Tivyside Advertiser* of 17 December, which reported that Effie Leah, one of the founders of the peace camp and among the first women to chain herself to the fence, and Cardigan's mayor, Mrs Frances Mason, had been amongst those taking part. The emphasis was again on 'ordinary women'.

It is apparent that women's movement groups in Wales were aware, and generally supportive, of Greenham from an early stage. For example, *Swansea Women's Centre Newsletter*, October/ November 1981, expressed support for the Greenham 'Peace March' (at this stage the name Greenham Common Women's Peace Camp was not yet in general use) and planned a visit of solidarity on 2 December; women were asked to donate tinned and dried food to take along. This newsletter also gave information about a young women's group, pregnancy-testing training, a Lesbian Line disco, and a WAVAW (Women Against Violence Against Women) conference that had taken place in Swansea. Clearly, support for the women's peace action was part of a whole range of activities which involved and supported women. Later, as Wales developed its own women's peace protests – actions at Royal Ordnance Factory, Llanishen, Cardiff, second WLFLOE march from Cardiff to Brawdy and the subsequent women's peace camps there, for example – local groups supported these too, but they also continued to support Greenham in many ways.

From 1983 on, as conditions worsened at Greenham, the women there were regularly intimidated by both the soldiers and local vigilantes. Shots were fired at them, their tents slashed and pigs' blood thrown at them; there were arson attempts and their cars and belongings damaged. Eventually, a system of night watches was established, where women who were not living at the camp arrived to sit up during the night and watch out for potential disturbances, to let the residents get some much needed sleep. Women in Cardiff, Newport and Swansea were on the rota of nightwatch volunteers, and Margery Lewis described how she would pick up women who had just finished work, who would drive down while she tried to get some sleep and then all keep watch during the night before she drove them back for work the next morning:

> It was an incredibly difficult time . . . and Greenham was terribly unpleasant . . . there was a Greenham smell, and when you'd been to Greenham you came back stinking because of the damp and the smoke from the fire . . . (Lewis, 1997, 4)

But in spite of this (and her chest being affected and feeling ill at times), she probably expressed a view many other women shared:

> . . . I think Greenham was a place where you felt comfortable. I mean, sometimes you didn't feel comfortable but by and large you were with women and you didn't feel that they were going to do something untoward that you wouldn't like . . . Greenham changed my life the

way it did so many other people . . . over the years I kept in touch with Greenham and sometimes I'd come out with really bad vibes and think I'm never going to go there again, and . . . about three or four days later back I went and I'd come away feeling great . . . when I went up I usually walked round the perimeter and usually somebody would come with me who I'd never met before and I nearly always took a pair of bolt clippers[4] up, not that I used them, I'd leave them there and you know they came in useful for somebody . . . (Lewis, 1997, 6)

Support from women frequently took the form of direct action. For example, *Swansea WONT Newsletter*, March 1983, reported that women had travelled from Swansea and Lampeter for the hearings on 15 and 16 February, at Newbury Magistrates' Court, of the 44 women arrested on New Year's Day for breaking into the base and dancing on the silos, an action caught in photographs which circulated the world. One of the women arrested was Carole Harwood, a veteran peace protestor from Cardiff, who, with around 35 other women, was sentenced to 14 days in Holloway. There is a substantial collection of documents relating to her experiences in The Feminist Archive, Bristol (and an account in Harford and Hopkins [1984]) which gives a horrifying picture of the conditions there and of the attitudes of those in authority.

The women from Swansea and Lampeter camped overnight at Green Gate, and a large number of women were arrested, including about eight of their party. Despite this they continued to blockade the base until another nine women were arrested. The same newsletter reported that four Swansea women went to Newbury to demonstrate at a visit by Michael Heseltine (then Secretary of State for Defence).

Two members of the group visited the base and 'arranged to be arrested'. They had pleaded not guilty, but were undecided about whether to pay the likely fine. This was a difficult question for many women involved in peace protests. Some of them, for a variety of reasons, did not feel able to risk imprisonment and so were left with little option but to pay up. *Swansea WONT Newsletter* for April 1983 described the court case:

One of them read a statement saying that having watched the previous days' trials they felt that proceedings were farcical and the verdict a foregone conclusion and that . . . they had decided to conduct their defence in the form of a comic opera.

The newsletter also noted that Swansea WONT group wanted to organise actions locally as well as supporting actions at Greenham (where it also continued to provide a night watch once a month) and in London.

Some of the organizers of the march later became deeply ambivalent about the direction Greenham was taking, and documents in the WFLOE, Margery Lewis and Carole Harwood Collections all underline these differences. One of the most divisive was the role of men at Greenham. The few men remaining at the camp were asked to leave in early February 1982. There have been various reasons given and the decision was disapproved of by some of the women as well as resented by the men; nevertheless it was agreed that men would be welcome to visit during the day but only women would live at the camp.

A letter in the WFLOE collection, written to Ann Pettitt from one of the men who took part in the Greenham march, illustrated some of the misconceptions and confusion around feminism:

Firstly I believe WFLOE is overtly a feminine cause. To my mind there is a distinct difference between 'feminine' and 'feminist' actions. The 'feminine' project smooth, flexible, persuasive pressures (female) and 'feminist' tend to be harsh, extreme, dogmatic pressures (male). If indeed the WFLOE is to prosper the latter elements I feel should be suppressed.

He goes on to suggest how future marches should be conducted:

Reject all singing and dancing throughout towns/villages – the more you look like refugees from a nuclear attack the better . . . Encourage women to wear dresses, skirts, smocks etc (anything but jeans) to promote a feminine image. (Anon, 1981)

Although there is no indication that these suggestions were shared by other men involved in peace actions, it is doubtful that many

women would have appreciated the suggestion that they chose
their clothes to appear more 'feminine' (apart from anything else,
issues of pure practicality dictated what to wear when on a peace
march when sleeping conditions were likely to be basic and there
would be few opportunities for washing clothes). It also showed a
total lack of awareness of the tactics (singing, dancing, street
theatre) so successfully used in actions such as the Women's
Pentagon Action in the USA.

Following the success of Embrace the Base, CND suggested
holding a mixed demonstration at Greenham in December 1983.
Ann Pettitt and a few of the Greenham 'originals' were in favour
of this, feeling that it was time for the peace movement as a whole
to become involved with Greenham. However, the women at the
camp, and many others involved in the peace movement, both
women and men, were strongly opposed to a mixed action. Letters
in the WFLOE collection express concerns about the likely
negative media reaction to any hint of splits within the peace
movement, and about the need to take notice of the wishes of the
women who were actually living at Greenham. Many suggested
that the peace movement was far from being split (Margery Lewis,
for example, wrote that 'we don't feel this in Cardiff') (Lewis,
1983), but that CND and mixed groups could arrange their own
protests while still supporting Greenham. Nevertheless, there were
certainly tensions between Greenham and CND, though it is likely
that the 'rank and file' members were generally more supportive
than the leadership. Other controversies concerned the lack of
black women, both at Greenham and in the peace movement as a
whole, and the growing visibility of lesbians.

Writing in *Spare Rib*, which devoted its May 1984 issue to the
women's peace movement, Elizabeth, a black woman, described
her immediate response to Greenham: 'I was ecstatic . . . meeting
so many women of all ages, actively working for the struggle
against the arms race, working against the negative acts of men.'
She suggested why black women were not more involved:

> . . . black people have many causes to fight for . . . fighting against
> racism and sexism, fascism, imperialism, unemployment, poor
> housing, capitalism . . . (Elizabeth, 1984, 19)

Lesbians were always present at Greenham (as they were, and are, everywhere else), becoming more visible as time passed. As Sara Roseneil pointed out:

> In the early days, sexuality was a line of fracture within Greenham, as some of the women who had been involved at the beginning believed that the predominance of lesbians at the camp should be played down, or even denied, and the presence of mothers and housewives – ordinary women – should be emphasised . . . Lesbians at the camp, particularly those who had come to Greenham already lesbian feminists, argued back not only that lesbians had a right to exist and take part in Greenham, but also that the politics of Greenham should recognise heterosexuality as oppressive of women . . . (Roseneil, 1995. 116)

To the right-wing media, of course, this was another excuse to rubbish Greenham and what it stood for.

Other Women's Peace Actions

Once the Greenham Women's Peace Camp was established, many women felt it was important to raise awareness of peace issues, and of Greenham, in their own communities. Women in Wales had been centrally involved in the formation of Greenham, and they continued to play a major role in the women's peace movement in Britain with a number of imaginative campaigns of their own.

'The Porth Women'

One of the most imaginative, though little reported, actions was the idea dreamt up by a group of five women from the Rhondda, who inevitably became known as 'the Porth Women'.

In November 1981, the five women, Susan Lamb, Christine King, Gaynor Hughes, Lynne Fortt and Leslie Rees decided to set up their own peace camp for a week in the centre of Porth, opposite the police station, as a gesture of support for those at Greenham Common. As the local paper, the *Rhondda Leader*,

reported, 'The five housewives plan to brave the cold and rain for
a week but hope to keep their protest colourful and friendly . . .
They are angry that their fellow nuclear campaigners in Newbury
had to actually chain themselves to the gates of a military base
before they were given any attention.' As their testimonies (for the
court case later brought in America against President Reagan)
made clear, they were unable to take part in the Cardiff to
Greenham march for a variety of reasons, but they were very
supportive of the camp, and concerned to bring the peace message
into their local community in an original and imaginative way
based on the idea of Greenham. There were anxieties, however,
and Anita Holmes, reporting on the action in *Arcade*, quoted Chris
King, who felt as she approached Porth Square, 'This is the
biggest mistake of my life'. Susan Lamb agreed, explaining in the
1985 film *I'll be here for all time* that the site was chosen because
all Valleys traffic converges there. In spite of wondering if they
would be arrested, by the first afternoon they had been given a
workmen's hut and numerous flasks of soup. During the evening a
man brought them a bottle of whisky explaining that his wife
would not let him go to sleep until he took something to keep them
warm. 'Every night people would come and talk to us. Women are
often intimidated by organizations like CND. They could identify
with us and would come and talk' (GWE 38-39). Public reaction
was generally very positive when they explained why they were
there, and they were visited by numerous CND groups and by
Michael Foot, who was visiting Wales at the time. Anita Holmes's
account concluded with the perceptive comment, 'The Rhondda's
history has been one of protest and political action, usually male
dominated. This latest demonstration, led by Rhondda women,
must be just the first in a series which goes to the heart of the local
community, making people aware that each of them can do
something about a threat that could engulf us all.'

Margery Lewis described learning of the Porth camp:

> We were up at Greenham and several of us stayed there. They had a
> caravan which was for the elderly so myself and Eunice Stallard were
> in this caravan . . . this was within the first few weeks of going to
> Greenham, and somebody came in and said 'guess what, the Porth

women have set up a camp in the middle of town'. So Eunice and I dashed down there . . . and there were the Porth women in a workmen's corrugated iron hut in the middle of town with all their banners and cartoons and things hanging round them . . .

She added that she always felt that the Porth women had been underestimated in accounts of Greenham.

Following this action, 'the Porth Women' became involved in Greenham. It was apparently their idea to get into the base and occupy the MOD sentry box, on 27 August 1982, as the Department of Transport was about to evict the camp. Nineteen women did so and were subsequently arrested and charged with intent to breach the peace. On 15 November 1982, 11 women, six of them Welsh, appeared at Newbury Magistrates' Court, where they hummed and swore on the Goddess. Their legal representatives claimed that their actions were legal since they were attempting to prevent genocide. More trials followed of women who had attempted to stop construction work on the base, and a total of 23, including nine from the Rhondda were sent to prison for two weeks. The media publicity helped to draw attention to the forthcoming Embrace the Base action.

Susan Lamb and Lynne Fortt wrote an account of their experiences in prison for *Welsh Rabbit – the newsletter of the Ecology Party in Wales*. Eleven of the 23 women imprisoned were held at East Side Park, near Maidstone. The governor, who claimed to be a pacifist herself, did her best to make conditions as pleasant as possible for them. They had lessons every day and one teacher gave up her class to allow an anti-nuclear video to be shown. As privileged prisoners, with the right to choose whether to work or not, they decided to work part-time and worked out a job-share rota, nine women sharing three gardening jobs. Susan Lamb 'took over the kitchens', starting proper vegetarian meals to replace the eggs and cheese which had previously been the only non-meat option on offer. The strict discipline began to be replaced as two or three women undertook the washing up while everyone else sang and danced. Between them, the Rhondda women clearly changed the atmosphere at this prison, helped of course by the governor's accommodating attitude.

The experience of another three Rhondda women, who were sent to Drake Hall Open Prison, was far less pleasant. They were ordered to work and when they refused were put in 'lock-up, two to a cell, for ten days'. Twelve women were eventually transferred during the night to four different closed prisons, including Holloway and Styall, the Home Office claiming that they were an unsettling influence. The *Times* of 27 November 1981 explained that a small peace camp had been set up outside and a picket had taken place. Demonstrations had also taken place outside East Sutton Park.

In November 1983 Susan Lamb, Lynne Fortt and Christine King, together with Carole Harwood and Liz Forder, Greenham and peace activists from Cardiff and a number of other women, were persuaded to take part in the 'Greenham against Cruise Missiles' court case in the USA. For the Porth women in particular this marked the start of disillusionment with the direction of the women's peace movement, in particular what they saw as an attempt at control. Documents in the Carole Harwood Collection in the Feminist Archive, Bristol, give a full account of this action, which was brought by using the Alien Tort Act, whereby any citizen in any country has a right to take legal action against the USA if his or her right to life is threatened by American policy. The women were supported by two American Congressmen, and they were also anxious to speak to groups of people throughout America to put pressure on them to condemn American policy.

Their criticism of the way the case was handled is clear. Five women involved were from Wales, five from England, only one of whom was based in London; but meetings were scheduled in London. One woman from Wales travelled with an eight-month-old baby. They were offered a clothes allowance:

> To many of the women from areas where living on the dole while trying to support your children was normal, the idea of spending a fixed sum on an outfit to make you appear acceptable to the American middle class has implications which were profoundly unsettling . . .

There were clearly two views of how the case should be presented: their lawyers were evidently anxious to project the correct image and choose 'acceptable' women to represent the camp; meanwhile the women from Wales clearly believed that although Greenham stood for questioning authority, they were being asked to conform to the views of 'experts'. In 1989, Carole Harwood published an article in *Peace News* in which Chris King, Lynne Fortt and Susan Lamb discussed with her the previous decade of peace activism and what might follow. In it, Susan Lamb suggested that the case had been fought to focus attention on the peace movement, not because the lawyers thought that they could win it. The women were there as symbols, not as Greenham women. If they had gone as Greenham women they might just have won (Harwood, 1989, 5).

In spite of their criticisms of this action, and the tactics used, it was evident that this group of working-class women from the Rhondda played an important role in the women's peace movement in Britain. They too illustrate the 'ordinary woman' paradox. To the *Rhondda Leader* they are housewives, and even *Radical Wales* prefaced an article by Jill Evans on Susan Lamb by saying that 'Susan Lamb is a married woman with two young daughters who lives in the Rhondda', though in this case it is used as a counterpoint to her radical peace work. This theme was further illustrated in the first of a two-part series in November 1982 on nuclear disarmament where the parents of four of the women were used to illustrate the diversity of the peace movement at this time:

> It is simple people like Mr Ronald Brinkworth . . . and his wife Audrey . . . of Porth, Rhondda, South Wales. Four of their seven daughters are now in prison for protesting against the American cruise missiles due to be sited at Greenham Common, Berkshire.

Royal Ordnance Factory, Llanishen, Cardiff

From the early 1960s, the Royal Ordnance Factory, Llanishen, had been involved in making components for nuclear warheads. It was the site of many actions during the 1980s, organised both by WFLOE and by CND.

For women and men in and around Cardiff, it represented an institution on their own doorstep which raised profound questions

about the manufacture of nuclear weapons and related environmental issues, as well as stirring economic debate on the provision
of jobs in such industries. During 1983, as well as picketing every
Friday morning from 7–8am as the day shift of workers entered
the site, WFLOE also organised a week long 'Peace Vigil' from
7–13 February. Women taking part kept a 'Vigil Diary' (now in the
National Library of Wales), written by different women as they
changed shifts. It presents a fascinating insight into the views of
some of the women who took part, and a snapshot of responses
from passers-by, local residents, workers and site and security
personnel. It begins, 'So many people have stopped this evening
that we thought we'd begin a vigil diary . . .'

The first entry records the unpleasant behaviour of a man who
tore their balloons from the wire and stamped on them suggesting
they should go to the Russian Embassy. By contrast, a young man
in a flash sports car gave them two bottles of wine to keep them
warm and a woman in another smart car offered chips and
expressed guilt that she wasn't with them.

Some local residents were friendly, offering free coffee and the
use of loos when required, and the diary suggests that some of the
initially hostile residents eventually thawed towards them. In her
interview with me in 1997, Margery Lewis was rather more cynical:

> . . . the Porth women were convinced that if you had a vigil down there
> that the whole locality, knowing what was contained and what was
> going on in that factory, would rise in arms and sympathise with what
> we were doing…nobody took any notice except to tell us to please
> clear out because we were being a nuisance and the value of their
> houses would go down. (Lewis, 1997, 4)

The diary points to a generally more positive response.

During the week, as well as talking about the implications of the
factory to anyone who would listen, the women also monitored
events on the site, noting car registration numbers, strange lights at
night and so on. A number of people expressed concern about the
possible health and environmental effects of the plant and the
women were given a number of reports of mysterious illnesses and
damage to property and crops.

Just as at Greenham, the women exposed the weaknesses in the security of the site by breaking in with a ladder. Another woman drove to the front gate in her car and was let in before being apprehended. Margery Lewis was called in by the police as someone had reported that she had a ladder in the back of her car but this was not pursued further, in her view because South Glamorgan Council had been declared a nuclear-free zone. (All county councils subsequently took similar action and in February 1982 Wales was declared the first nuclear-free country in Europe). The ROF's location in a nuclear-free zone was, however, irrelevant since it was under the control of central government.

The tensions within the women's peace movement over the rationale for women-only actions and adherence (or not) to them, are visible in the accounts in the diary. For example, during the week, Anne Pettitt told the group that she was sending a batch of home-made soup with a man who previously had had little contact with the women's movement; the women were asked to be nice to him. A later entry reported that he duly arrived and sat for much of the night talking to the women, so presumably they didn't frighten him away. The fact that the comment about 'being nice' was made at all showed an awareness that some women would not welcome a man, particularly one not used to feminist ideas, into the middle of a women's action.

Another entry is even more pointed:

Lynne and I are disturbed by this element of extreme feminism, or extremism of any kind. Our only purpose is to ban nuclear weapons to achieve peace for everybody. We're disturbed by reports of aggressive feminists at Greenham (who, we know, are refusing valuable offers of help, money, support – especially from men – the Peace movement needs help from every source). We think a deputation – perhaps of 'Greenham veterans' – should go to Greenham to talk to the women. It would be tragic if all the good done in the last year is lost, because of a few extremists amongst us. (Vigil Diary, 1983)

The links between feminism and the peace movement, '[the] profound relationship between the fact that individual women are commonly attacked and beaten up and that a nuclear war threatens the entire world' (Feminism & Nonviolence Study Group, 1983), were clearly missing here.

Later that year, on 24 May 1983, Hiroshima Day, as part of a series of events, two women peace protestors, Carole Harwood and Dianne Dodd, climbed onto the roof of the sentry box. Women circled below, handing out flowers to the police. Carole Harwood and Dianne Dodd were arrested for 'threatening behaviour', but the charge was later dropped. The protestors made the obvious point that they were not the threat, but rather the ROF by manufacturing nuclear materials. They pledged to continue protesting. The *Western Mail* quoted them: '. . . we have made the people of Cardiff aware that here is a factory making nuclear materials and that it is a threat to the whole city' (*Western Mail*, 1983).

The Brawdy March and Women's Peace Camps

Another significant action of the women's peace movement in Wales was the march and peace camps at Brawdy, the US nuclear tracking station near Newgale in Pembrokeshire. The march was organised by WFLOE following the Greenham march, and took place from 27 May to 5 June 1982.

At the same time, evictions were taking place at Greenham, and the Falklands War, which lasted 74 days from March till June, received jingoistic support from some of the tabloid newspapers.

It was not, in fact, the first peace march to Brawdy. In 1981, Nigel Jenkins reported in *Arcade* on the two-mile march from Newgale to Brawdy organised by CND. He complained about what he saw as the tokenist treatment of the Welsh language but concluded that this was because most of the CND activists appeared to be English, and was dismissive of 'one woman speaker (a Londoner living in Carmarthen) [who] wondered where the other women speakers were . . .' (Jenkins, 1981).

A letter in the WFLOE Collection from Monica Sjoo, a well-known (and sometimes controversial) artist then living near Fishguard, to Ann Pettitt commented that there had been no women's banners on that march. (Monica made a banner for the

WFLOE march however). Clearly, women were not significant in the peace movement at this time, and it was to be Greenham which began to change that.

Although it received some publicity from local newspapers, alternative magazines and (of course) the women's movement media in Wales, Brawdy has otherwise received little attention.

A journalist from the alternative magazine *Rebecca* went on the march and her detailed report appeared in July 1982. It was about twice the size of the Cardiff-Greenham march with around 75 women, six men and 20 children taking part. Val Allen, in *Touch and Go*, estimated that about half were Welsh and the rest were mainly from England and Scotland, plus one each from America, France and Holland (Allen 1982). Following the Greenham march, WFLOE intended the Brawdy one to visit as many communities as possible, including speaking to local peace and women's groups, and planned a route through some of the Welsh mining communities. At Pontypridd (the first night's stop) they were invited into the chamber of the new mayor of Rhondda. The *Rebecca* account described '100 hot sweaty women and children surrounded by mayoral splendour'; at the evening reception the mayor apparently made a joke about rape, not surprisingly less than enthusiastically received by the marchers.

Despite the Women's Liberation Movement of the 1970s and the role of women in Wales, the Welsh valleys were still essentially conservative in the roles played by women, and this led to a significant pattern emerging on the march. At each stop women from the chapels, the Labour Party, CND groups and Merched y Wawr prepared and served food while men made speeches and sometimes even caried the marchers' banners.

There were different views on this among the marchers. Some felt that women should confront the view of a male-dominated world as part of the challenge to the nuclear age. Others felt that as they were visiting very traditional societies, it would be rude to challenge things. At one stop one marcher, 'Dee, a lecturer from Penarth' (Deirdre Beddoe, later Emeritus Professor at the University of Glamorgan, and one of the pioneers of the history of women in Wales) arrived early at the lunch-stop and spoke to the women. 'I told them how much I would like them to speak to us –

rather than it just being the men as usual.' After a lot of encouragement, the local primary school headmistress agreed to speak (*Rebecca*, 1982, 16–18).

This pattern was, of course, completely overturned only two years later with the emergence of the Women's Support Groups in the 1984–85 Miners' Strike, when women from these communities finally found a voice. During this period too, women from the mining communities were regular visitors to Greenham. It can be argued that it was the women's peace movement, particularly the examples of the Porth camp, and the Brawdy march, which began to change these women.

Poet and writer Janet Dubé also went on the march. She later wrote about her impressions in *Touch & Go*:

> . . . we were for a few days passed from one mining or ex-mining community to another . . . [leaving Onllwyn Welfare Hall] . . . one local woman told me that the event had brought together people who otherwise might not have co-operated; groceries had been offered and used from over the length of the Dulais valley.' She added 'I was more aware of the history of dissent during those two hours than at any other time or place over the whole journey. The whole walk was a series of exchanges between communities, life styles, generations and politics. (Dubé, 1983, 19)

During the march, the walkers discussed what to do when they arrived at Brawdy. They decided that some of them would blockade the base, staying there for six days to coincide with President Reagan's visit to London. On the Friday, around 40 women and a few children left the march to begin the blockade, and 20 remained until the following Thursday. On the Wednesday, 13 women chained themselves to the anchor in front of the base. There were no arrests during the blockade. Susan Lamb left the blockade to travel to London to address the rally in Hyde Park, telling the crowd of 250,000, 'If every one of you put your bodies outside a US base now we would have no Cruise missiles' (Allen, 1982). The following year, on 24 May, 1983, a women's peace camp was set up at Brawdy. It was timed to take place over the Bank Holiday weekend, and unlike Greenham, which happened by accident, this was a carefully planned camp. Around 50 women and children took part, and Sunday 27 was designated as a Fancy Dress Party. This was part of the rationale: face the monstrous apparatus of war with something life-affirming and fun. *Swansea WONT Newsletter*, April 1983, reported 'From 24th May there will be a women's peace camp at Brawdy . . . we thought a women's peace camp at Brawdy would be a focus in Wales . . .'

The camp was set up again the following year, apparently for the whole summer. *Touch and Go* reported in November on attempts to take down the perimeter fence. The summer of 1986 also saw a women's peace camp here, described in *The Guardian* as 'a Greenham Common-style peace camp'. A number of women were arrested for tying a banner to the fence under byelaws which had recently been passed to prohibit trespass and interference. Unfortunately, unlike Greenham, information about the Brawdy peace camps is relatively sparse.

Conclusion

Since the 1980s, although less visible, the movement has continued worldwide. In 2005, amongst the many protests against Britain's decision to join the US in the war against Iraq, 75 women, many of them elderly and including some in their eighties, demonstrated outside the main gate of USAF Fairford. The group included eight women from west Wales, among them two of the organisers of the Cardiff to Greenham march, Ann Pettitt and Karmen Thomas (formerly Cutler). A letter was circulated to potential supporters (which also appeared on a section of a Newcastle Emlyn website devoted to the Stop the War Campaign):

> This letter comes to you from the two women . . . who organised the women's march from Cardiff to Greenham Common in 1981. Because we were ignored then, the peace camp began and all the subsequent actions and demonstrations made the world listen. Together, thousands of women did change history.

It goes on to explain the proposed Fairford action:

> We wish to act as women because we have a history and a culture of
> effective action, because there are many thousands of ex-Greenham
> women still willing, we hope, to give their creative energy to stopping
> war; and there are many thousands of younger women, and would-be
> Greenham women, who have never experienced first-hand the unique
> strength and power of a women's action for peace. We know we can
> organise quickly, without fuss, bureaucracy or hierarchies; we can act
> with dignity and care for each other and we know we can
> communicate . . . Let's make the difference. (Pettitt 2005)

Clearly, some of the women involved in the women's peace
movement in Wales are still actively campaigning. Others are
active in other ways, particularly in women's organisations of all
kinds, and in working for what they see as a more just society.

NOTES

[1] See, for example, Roseneil, *Disarming Patriarchy*; Onlywomen Press, *Breaching the Peace*; Feminism & Nonviolence Study Group, *Piecing it Together*.

[2] Jane Hutt, who has been a member of the Cabinet since the formation of the Wales Assembly Government in 2000, also stood (unsuccessfully) as a Labour Party candidate for Cardiff North in this election. She campaigned on the twin issues of jobs and peace.

[3] A letter in the WFLOE Collection dated 8.9.81 to Ann Pettitt and her partner assumed that she would be back 'and settled down again after the obviously big domestic upheaval of the march. We hope it went well though found it unreported in the *Guardian* and *Sunday Times*, perhaps it was picked up elsewhere?'

[4] Bolt-cutters were mainly used to cut through the perimeter fence in order to gain access to the base, which happened regularly.

BIBLIOGRAPHY

Allan, Val. 'Why a women's march', *Touch & Go*. August, 1982.

Anon. 'Letter to Ann Pettitt'. Cardiff, Glamorgan Record Office, WFLOE Collection, 1981.

Anon. *What I did on my holiday*. Bristol, Feminist Archive, Carole Harwood Collection, 1983.

Bangor Women's Enterprise Network. *Wales Women's Directory*, Bangor. WEB, 1984.

Beddoe, Deirdre. *Out of the shadows: a history of women in twentieth-century Wales*. Cardiff: University of Wales Press, 2000.

Blackwood, Caroline. *On the Perimeter: Caroline Blackwood at Greenham Common*. London: Flamingo, 1984.

Campbell, Thalia (n.d.). *100 Years of Women's Banners*. Bristol, Women for Life on Earth, Art and Publicity and Arts for Labour Wales.

Cook, Alice & Kirk, Gwyn. *Greenham Women Everywhere: dreams, ideas and actions from the women's peace movement*. London: Pluto Press, 1983.

Daily Express, 8th January 1983.

Dubé, Janet. 'Mine of information', *Touch and Go* (34).16 July–19 August 1983.

Elizabeth. Black woman's reaction. London: *Spare Rib* (142), May 1984.

Evans, Sian. Letter in WFLOE Collection. Cardiff, Glamorgan Record Office, 1983.

Feminism, and Nonviolence Study Group. *Piecing it together: feminism and nonviolence*. Westwood Ho! Devon: 1983.

Graham, Helen [*et al.*] (eds.). *The Feminist Seventies*. York: Raw Nerve Books, 2003.

Harford, Barbara & Hopkins, Sarah. *Greenham Common: Women at the Wire*. London: The Women's Press, 1984.

Harwood, Carole. 'Back in the Rhondda'. *Peace News* 9 June 1989.

Heath, Tony. 'Peace women arrested at base'. *The Guardian* 26 August 1986.

Holmes, Anita. 'Chain Action'. Cardiff: *Arcade* (28), 11 December 1981.

I'll be here for all time. Video, Wales, Boadicea Films, 1985.

Jenkins, Nigel. *Arcade*, (16), 12 June 1981.

Jolly, Margaretta. *After the Seventies: Greenham Common Women and Dreams of a Common Language*. In Graham, Helen [*et al.*] (eds.), The Feminist Seventies. York: Raw Nerve Books, 2003.

Jones, Lynne. (ed). *Keeping the Peace: Women's Peace Handbook 1*. London: The Women's Press, 1983.

Kanter, Hannah [*et.al*] (eds.). *Sweeping Statements: writings from the Women's Liberation Movement 1981–83*. London: The Women's Press, 1984.

Lewis, Margery. Unpublished interview with Avril Rolph for South Wales History and Archive Project, Pontypridd, University of Glamorgan, 1997.

Liddington, Jill. *The Long Road to Greenham: feminism and anti-militarism in Britain since 1920*. London: Virago, 1989.

Lovenduski, Joni & Randall, Vicky (eds.).*Contemporary Feminist Politics: women and power in Britain*. Oxford: Oxford University Press, 1992.

Lynchcombe (n.d.) *At least Cruise is clean*. Newbury: Niccolo Press, 1984?

Onlywomen Press. *Breaching the Peace: a collection of radical feminist papers*. London: Onlywomen Press, 1983.

Osmond, John. 'Life guards at the gates of Greenham Common'. Cardiff: *Arcade* (26) 13 November 1981.

Pettitt, Ann. *Feminism for her own good*. Nottingham, WIRES: the national women's liberation newsletter (101) November 1980.

Pettitt, Ann. 'Fighting the nuclear menace'. Cardiff: *Arcade* (20) 7 August 1981.

Pettitt, Ann. Fairford Airforce Base. [Accessed 14/10/2005].

Rebecca. 'The Road to peace'. Cardiff: *Rebecca* July 1982.

'Women's Nuclear Protest'. *Rhondda Leader*, 11 November 1981.

Rolph, Avril. *A Movement of its own: the Women's Liberation Movement in South Wales* in Graham, Helen (*et al*) (ed.) The Feminist Seventies. York: Raw Nerve Books, 2003.

Roseneil, Sasha. *Disarming Patriarchy: feminism and political action at Greenham*. Buckingham: Open University Press, 1995.

Swansea WONT Group. *Newsletter*, April 1983

Wales Women's Directory (1984).

Western Mail. 8 August 1983.

Young, Alison. *Femininity in dissent*. London: Routledge, 1990.

DEVOLUTION: A VIEW FROM THE RIGHT

Nick Bourne

Since 1997, Welsh Conservatives have made a remarkable journey. From a position of opposition to Welsh devolution, and without Welsh representation in Parliament, the party is now a resurgent force in Wales. With Welsh MPs at Westminster and a successful and hard-working group in the Welsh Assembly, the party has turned its fortunes around. A commitment to devolution and localism will bring further success in the future.

The party political manifestos for the May general election in 1997 set the stage for a summer of campaigning on the issue of Welsh devolution. The Labour party was fully committed to a referendum on a National Assembly for Wales:

> We will meet the demand for decentralisation of power to Scotland and Wales, once established in referendums. Subsidiarity is as sound a principle in Britain as it is in Europe. Our proposal is for devolution not federation. A sovereign Westminster Parliament will devolve power to Scotland and Wales. The Union will be strengthened and the threat of separatism removed. As soon as possible after the election, we will enact legislation to allow the people of Scotland and Wales to vote in separate referendums on our proposals, which will be set out in white papers. These referendums will take place not later than the autumn of 1997 . . . The Welsh assembly will provide democratic control of the existing Welsh Office functions. It will have secondary legislative powers and will be specifically empowered to reform and democratise the quango state.[1]

Both the Liberal Democrats and Plaid Cymru had long called for the devolution of power from Westminster. In their 1997 manifestos, the Liberal Democrats called for 'home rule for Wales with the creation of a Welsh Senedd', while Plaid went even further, proposing that once a Welsh parliament was in place, Wales would 'move forward to full self-government'.[2] The Conservative party disagreed. Opposed to the proposals for a Welsh Assembly, the Conservative manifesto summarized its position:

> The Union between Scotland, Wales and Northern Ireland and England underpins our nation's stability. The Conservative commitment to the United Kingdom does not mean ignoring the distinctive individuality of the different nations. On the contrary, we have gone further in recognising that diversity than any previous government . . . the development of new assemblies in Scotland and Wales would create strains which could well pull apart the Union. That would create a new form of government which would be hungry for power. It would risk rivalry and conflict between these Parliaments or Assemblies and the Parliament at Westminster. And it would raise serious questions about whether the representation of Scottish and Welsh MPs at Westminster – and their role in matters affecting English affairs – could remain unchanged. Nor do we believe it would be in the interests of the Scottish or Welsh people.[3]

Labour's win in the 1997 general election meant the battle for Welsh devolution had begun in earnest.

1997 Referendum & the No Campaign

The 'Just Say No' campaign was fought on a shoestring budget. I was a part of that campaign. Other key figures in the campaign were Jonathan Evans, Gwilym Jones and Nigel Evans but, although Conservative-led, the campaign had the notable support of individuals from other parties. Betty Bowen and Carys Pugh, Labour stalwarts from the Rhondda, were heavily involved and advice was given by Labour's Viscount Tonypandy (the former George Thomas). Assistance came from Julian and Robert Hodge through their association with the Bank of Wales. Media work tended to be done by me and Tim Williams, a London-based former Labour activist, from Cardiff, and by Jonathan Evans from London. The Just Say No campaign was pitted against the combined might of the party machines of Welsh Labour, Plaid

Cymru and the Welsh Liberal Democrats. The support of prominent figures such as Ron Davies, Peter Hain and Win Griffiths from Labour, Dafydd Wigley for Plaid Cymru and Richard Livsey from the Liberal Democrats, plus various celebrities, meant that the 'Yes for Wales' campaign was a strong, indeed formidable, force. The general election was also still fresh in people's minds. Labour was riding high following their landslide victory; Conservatives, meanwhile, were coming to terms with the fact they no longer had any Welsh MPs at Westminster. Even though devolution had been rejected convincingly in 1979, the political landscape in 1997 meant that this was an altogether different situation.

In many ways it was a David and Goliath contest. The government spent around £1m on publicity for the new Assembly, with information on their White Paper *A Voice for Wales* distributed to every household before the referendum.[4] By contrast, the No campaign had no institutional organizations, no large battalions backing it and no network of the great and the good. As the *Financial Times* put it on the day of the vote, 'while there's nothing wrong with touring rural Wales in an old Leyland bus, it's not much of a draw when the other side has got the PM pressing flesh and kissing babies.'[5]

A week before the Welsh vote, on 11 September, a referendum was held on Scottish devolution. The result was decisive: 74.3 per cent voted in favour of a Scottish Parliament. It was widely believed that Wales would follow suit – although not, perhaps, as resoundingly. The Secretary of State for Wales, Ron Davies, said, 'If we don't grasp the opportunity, Wales could be, in two or three years' time, the only part of the country ruled by diktat from London in the old way.'[6] Yet, to the surprise of many, the Welsh No campaign came within a hair's breadth of victory. The referendum was held on 18 September 1997. As the day approached, the media began to warn that the result was far from certain and polling suggested that it would be much closer than first expected.[7] Devolution was won by the narrowest of margins: 50.3 percent voted in favour, 49.7 per cent were against. Fifty per cent of the Welsh electorate failed to turn out. The death of Princess Diana, at the end of August, may conceivably have played a part in the final outcome. There had been a standstill in campaigning and the mourning of the Princess evoked a strong sense of Britishness amongst Welsh people. Nonetheless, the people of Wales had voted for a Welsh Assembly.

The nuts and bolts of how the Assembly would operate needed to be determined. A few months after the referendum, in December 1997, Ron Davies set up the National Assembly Advisory Group (NAAG). The NAAG comprised political representatives and others, appointed to prepare guidelines for the workings of the new Assembly and lay the foundations for the Assembly's standing orders. It was a constructive process, with a consensual and effective chairman, John Elfed Jones, the former chair of the Welsh Language Board. The Conservative appointed onto the committee by Ron Davies was Viscount St Davids. He had not been put forward by the Conservative party but had campaigned for a Yes vote. St Davids was of blue blood but proved an extremely able and effective contributor to NAAG. Michael Ancram also put forward my name and Ron Davies duly accepted the nomination. The other members were: Eluned Morgan, MEP for Mid & West Wales (Labour); Helen Mary Jones, the then Vice-chair of Plaid Cymru and Deputy Director of the Equal Opportunities Commission; Kirsty Williams, Vice-president of the Welsh Liberal Democrats; Ken Hopkins, ex-Chair of the Labour Party Policy Commission and a former Director of Education for Mid Glamorgan Council; the late Ioan Bowen Rees, former Chief Executive of Gwynedd County Council; Mari James, Vice-chair of the Yes for Wales campaign and a former lecturer in the University of Wales; Joyce Redfern, the then Chief Executive of Monmouthshire Council; Howard Marshall, Policy Officer for UNISON; the late Ian Spratling, the then Vice-chair of CBI Wales; Marjory Dykins, Chair of the Wales Council for Voluntary Action; and Ray Singh, of the Commission for Racial Equality.

NAAG considered how the full Assembly should operate, what roles should be given to the First Secretary (later the First Minister), what matters should be conducted by the Executive Committee (later the Cabinet); also the role of Assembly secretaries (later ministers), subject committees and the role of the Presiding Officer. The group also explored how European issues should be tackled, how an equality agenda could be catered for, as well as matters of standards, the Assembly budget and other related issues. Detailed discussion took place on all theses issues and, in general, a consensual way forward was found. Certainly, by the time that the report was signed off in August 1998, members were able to agree on a report that formed the basis for the Government of Wales Bill, which later became the Act of 1998. The principal amendment made to the Bill as it went through Parliament was largely prompted by the NAAG's recommendations. This was that it was not feasible to have a Cabinet made up of Chairs of each of the subject committees with, therefore, an all-party Cabinet. It was felt more appropriate to have a traditional Cabinet formed by the governing party, and this was then incorporated into the Bill. It was crucial that Conservatives played a positive role in these formative stages.

With the opening of the new Assembly in May 1999, the Conservative group needed to elect a leader. Rod Richards and I ran for the leadership in November 1998. In a ballot of Welsh party members, Rod Richards received 58 per cent of the vote compared to 42 per cent for myself, with a 49 percent turnout. Rod Richards's leadership signalled a much more aggressive style of politics. In many ways this was a gift to the Labour party, who were able to characterize the Conservative group as unchanged despite their 1997 defeat.

At Westminster, with William Hague as Conservative leader, there was swift acceptance in Conservative high command of the significance of the devolution result. Conservatives should concentrate on making the Assembly work for the people of Wales. That has been the tenor ever since. However, in the May 1999 elections many, including Rod Richards, seemed to sense an opportunity to re-run the referendum campaign. As a result, a significant number of Conservative voters stayed at home and the party received only 16 per cent of the vote – slipping from being the second party in Wales to third, behind Plaid Cymru. Labour won 28 seats, Plaid Cymru 17, Conservatives nine and the Liberal Democrats six. The Conservatives had underperformed. Critics foresaw a sea change in Welsh politics, with the nationalists surging forward as the Conservatives were pushed to the margins.

It was perhaps to be expected that the first few months of the Assembly would be a turbulent time for all parties. The combative and hostile style adopted by the Conservative group in the initial stages meant that it was difficult to exploit the full potential of a Labour party struggling with a minority government and leadership problems. The issue that would dominate the early days of the first Assembly term was whether the Treasury would find the money to match the £1.3 billion European Objective One funding for west Wales and the Valleys, or whether it would have to come out of the Assembly's block grant. In a Plaid Cymru motion, debated on 14 July 1999, Conservatives voted with Plaid and the Liberal Democrats against a key Labour amendment on the issue of Objective One funding. As the Institute of Welsh Affairs described it, this was 'a harbinger of further skirmishes'.[8] It was also the earliest example of opposition parties putting aside their differences to defeat Labour.

In August 1999, Rod Richards resigned as Conservative leader following allegations of assault and I took over as leader – having received the unanimous backing of Welsh Conservative AMs. There was a real opportunity for the party to adopt a fresh approach and reposition itself in the new political landscape. A more understanding and moderate approach was imperative. For the long term, this meant that, ironically, the very institution opposed by the Conservatives, now offered the party a chance to renew itself in Wales. Welsh politics needed a centre-right party that could offer positive ideas for the future of the country. It was an opportunity not to be lost. In the short term, it meant closer working with opposition parties in the face of a minority Labour administration.

On 2 November 1999, Conservatives put down a motion of No Confidence in the First Secretary, Alun Michael. This was, in the first instance, due to his failure to act over the censure of his Agricultural Secretary but also for his Government's continuing failure to act as a minority government, turning a blind eye to pressing issues like the health budget and Objective One. Other opposition parties did not support the motion on that occasion. However, the next day, opposition parties worked together to produce a joint statement calling for additional funding from the

Treasury to ensure EU funds. In the months that followed, the First Secretary was pressed time and again on the issue of Objective One funding.

On 9 February 2000, a vote of No Confidence in Alun Michael was passed. Tabled jointly by Plaid Cymru, the Welsh Conservatives and Liberal Democrats, it was brought about by the failure of the First Secretary to secure Objective One funding from the UK government. It was clear that the Labour party had put cordial relations with Westminster ahead of Wales's interests. Alun Michael enjoyed the confidence of Tony Blair but in a devolved Wales the appointment had backfired. As I said to Plenary, 'The First Secretary gives the impression that Tony Blair only has to say "jump" and he will ask "how high?". Wales needs someone to fight for these vital match funds from Westminster.'[9] It is interesting to look back at the germs of opposition collaboration in the very first months of the Assembly. Welsh parties were quickly forced to come to terms with the day-to-day realities of the new constitutional settlement. In the space of a few short months, Conservatives were busy turning around their fortunes and showing the people of Wales they would work hard to make the Assembly a success. Today, opposition collaboration on an almost daily basis on the Assembly's budget and minority party debates has been similarly born out of the need for an alternative to Labour failure.

At this time there was much discussion in corridors and Assembly offices as to who was likely to succeed Alun Michael. To me, it was always obvious that there was only one person who would emerge from the largest party: Rhodri Morgan. However, I certainly recall Mike German, the Liberal Democrat leader, coming to me to canvass the possibility of Ron Davies. I pointed out the very obvious difficulty to Mike that Ron would not be the Labour party choice and that it was for Labour, as the governing party at that stage, to put forward their preferred candidate. Rhodri had been denied the crown twice. Interestingly, Peter Hain had run the campaigns of both Ron Davies and then Alun Michael, but later he worked alongside Rhodri Morgan, one as First Minister and the other as Secretary of State for Wales.

On coming into office, Rhodri Morgan undertook a minor cabinet reshuffle. Taking the post of First Minister and Economic

Development himself, he brought Sue Essex into the Cabinet as Environment Secretary. She had long been an ally of Rhodri Morgan's.

In the autumn of 2000, Rhodri Morgan and Mike German did a deal and entered into a period of partnership government. Mike German became Deputy First Minister and another Liberal Democrat, Jenny Randerson, entered the Cabinet as Culture Minister. Tom Middlehurst resigned as Minister as soon as he knew that a Lib/Lab pact had been signed off and subsequently Peter Law and Rosemary Butler were removed from office, making way for the two Liberal Democrats. Jane Davidson joined the Cabinet as Education Minister. She thus relinquished her post as Deputy Presiding Officer. There then followed a battle for the succession to the Deputy Presiding Office. The Labour party had taken it for granted that its nominee, Rosemary Butler, would succeed, but Plaid Cymru and the Welsh Conservatives quickly got together to ensure that this was not seen as a Labour gift. There was discussion of an alternative candidate and the opposition parties settled on John Marek, who was subsequently elected in a secret ballot. At that stage, of course, he was still a Labour AM.

Undoubtedly, the partnership government provided more stability than had previously been the case. The government was now assured of a majority in Assembly dealings and a period of relatively stable government continued for the remainder of the Assembly term, despite the temporary standing down from office by the Liberal Democrat Leader because of questions involving expenses relating to his former employment in the Welsh Joint Education Committee. Once these matters were cleared up, Mike German then returned to the partnership cabinet.

With the Liberal Democrats and Labour in a coalition, it fell to Plaid Cymru and the Welsh Conservatives to provide the opposition. Despite being the official opposition party, Plaid Cymru failed to capitalize fully on their electoral success in the first Assembly term. In 2001, Dafydd Wigley resigned following ill health, and in many ways that period signalled the beginning of Plaid's difficulties. Dafydd Wigley had long been a well-liked and respected political figure. With Dafydd's ill health and other internal party problems, Plaid was losing the momentum it had gained in 1999. When Dafydd retired, alongside Cynog Dafis and Phil Williams, in 2003, the party was left without three big hitters. The void they left undoubtedly created a further opportunity for the Welsh Conservatives.

Second Assembly

In the 2003 elections Welsh Conservatives made significant strides forward. The party secured two extra seats and was the only party to increase its share of the vote in every electoral region. Importantly, two female Welsh Conservative AMs were elected. Welsh Conservatives had an extra spring in their step.

One of the policies in the programme of the partnership government had been to commission a review of powers and electoral processes of the Welsh Assembly. This task was entrusted to Ivor Richard, a Labour peer of known independence and ability. The Welsh Conservatives were asked to make a nomination to the Richard Commission and duly did so. Paul Valerio, a close associate of mine, and a former Vice-chairman of the party in Wales, was duly nominated as the Welsh Conservative choice to the Richard Commission.

With the publication of the Richard Commission in 2004, it was also important for Welsh Conservatives to revisit constitutional questions. The main arguments against devolution were founded on the threat to the Union and on the cost of devolved politics. On the former, these concerns have been largely allayed. There is currently no real threat to the union and the nationalist party, Plaid Cymru, has seen support dwindle. Certainly Plaid's prospects have been hampered by leadership questions and internal divisions but nevertheless it is fair to say that there is very little public thirst for their long-term aim – for Wales to break away from the UK. On the contrary, one of the main beneficiaries of devolution has been the Welsh Conservatives, a unionist party.

On the issue of cost, time has shown that there was justified cause for concern. In 1997, the CBI Wales warned the Commons Welsh Affairs Select Committee about the inevitable increase in bureaucracy and the cost that the Assembly would bring.[10] The people of Wales were not properly informed about the likely cost of devolution. In fact, Kevin Morgan, who was part of the executive running the Yes campaign, has acknowledged that 'it was more expensive than we had originally thought'.[11] It is true to say the costs have soared. Despite Labour claiming that devolution would only cost an extra £15–20m a year, in 2002 it emerged that the running cost of the Assembly was £148m, more than twice the amount spent in the final year before devolution – in part due to the net increase of 220 civil servants and the 60 Assembly Members.[12] The so-called 'bonfire of the quangos' which, it was argued, would offset the cost of devolution, did not materialize until 2004, when the First Minister announced that several Assembly-sponsored public bodies would be brought in-house.[13] It is still unclear whether there will be benefits from some of the merger plans. It was a seemingly rushed decision, without prior notice given to the heads of the organizations involved and time will tell whether the proposals have been properly thought through. Certainly the decision to bring in the Welsh Language Board and parts of the Arts Council in-house has been vehemently opposed by Welsh Conservatives as politicization of the Welsh language and culture which should be kept at arm's length. The ditching of the well-known brands of the Welsh Development Agency and Wales Tourist Board may also cost Wales dear. Perhaps the most obvious example of massive cost has been the building of a new Assembly chamber in Cardiff Bay. This venture has hardly engendered love in the Welsh public for their new institution despite the very obvious grandeur and impressive iconic status of that new building.

Aside from areas of waste, some costs were of course to be expected with the associated demands of a new institution. However, it is hard to see why the cost of the Wales Office has more than doubled. The Wales Office budget has burgeoned to nearly £5m, with a rising payroll of staff, even though most of its powers and responsibilities have been devolved to Cardiff.[14] When the responsibilities of the Wales Office have been reduced, these escalating costs are troubling. Ensuring public money is spent wisely will remain one of the Welsh Conservatives' chief concerns. Scrutiny of budgets and keeping waste down are important responsibilities for all AMs.

That said, devolution has brought important advantages. The investment in the Assembly by interest groups, charities and other public bodies means that it would be a tremendous waste of time, money and energy to turn the clock back now. The availability and immediacy of Welsh politicians to the public is an obvious benefit. An emphasis on openness and transparency is also positive.

Even though the Assembly has faced an uphill battle to convince the Welsh nation that it is a positive step forward for Wales, opinion polls suggest that support for devolution has grown since 1999. As the Richard Commission found, people are critical of the Assembly and want it to perform better but most do not want it scrapped.[15] Blame for the failure to tackle some of Wales's most pressing issues, like lengthy hospital waiting lists and poor rates of economic competitiveness, lies squarely with the Labour Government in Cardiff rather than the institution itself. With support for devolution growing and the current settlement unsustainable in the long-term, the arguments in favour of law-making powers for the Assembly are persuasive. This does not mean rushing headlong into more constitutional upheaval, but it does mean looking seriously at how we can achieve a lasting settlement.

During the No campaign, William Hague, as Conservative party leader, said that Wales would get the worst of both worlds: a loss of influence at UK level but with no real power over its own affairs.[16] He was right. The constitutional imbalance between Wales and Scotland was hard to justify and Labour legislation has done nothing to provide for a permanent workable settlement. Labour's new Government of Wales Bill offers little hope of a clear way forward. My own preference is for a legislative parliament, although not necessarily within the timescale suggested by the Richard Commission report. If primary legislative powers are proposed then the Welsh people should have the final say in a referendum.

The political landscape has changed and the argument has moved on. Abolishing the Assembly is not an option. The question is how we can ensure that it delivers more effectively for the people of Wales. What policies should be pursued and what does the future hold for the Welsh Conservatives?

Under the leadership of Iain Duncan Smith, the policy of positive engagement largely continued, although 'noises off' from dissident members occurred from time to time and were occasionally reflected by the contribution of some AMs. Under Michael Howard's leadership the party opted for a preferendum approach which allowed individuals within the party to campaign for the status quo, additional powers or indeed the abolition of the Assembly. This was widely seen as untenable in the long term, particularly with the loss of the 2005 election, meaning that the Conservative party was likely to be out of power for another four years at Westminster.

With the arrival of David Cameron as leader, the party moved on. As many commentators suggested, the party has faced its Clause 4 moment. With a leader who shares a similar approach to devolution, I was able to ensure that the devolution settlement was accepted and indeed the party did not rule out endorsing additional powers for the Assembly. This more positive approach to devolution sat much more comfortably with the nature of Welsh politics in the first decade of the 21st century, with all polls suggesting a growing acceptance of the Assembly and a larger number of people wanting a similar settlement to that in Scotland. The party had returned to its pragmatic roots and away from the ideological approach to politics that had characterized the period of opposition from 1997 to the end of 2005.

Welsh Conservatives have committed themselves to working hard to make the Assembly work for the people of Wales. This has meant a fresh look at policies, finding ways to improve Welsh public services and the economy. It was also vital to ensure a renewed emphasis on preserving and promoting Welsh culture and language. Conservatives have done a great deal for the Welsh language, establishing S4C, the Welsh Language Board, and the development of Welsh-medium education. Notwithstanding, it has been to the detriment of the Conservatives in Wales that they have been considered to some degree as an 'English party'. It was clear that there was a real need to shake off this image, to define Conservative Welshness while, at the same time, remaining true to unionist credentials. For sometime now, Conservatives in Wales have become known as the Welsh Conservatives – with an extra accent on the 'Welsh'. The party has its own Director, headquarters and emblem but, most importantly, Welsh Conservative policies on devolved issues are made in Wales. In October 2003, I spoke at a Welsh Conservative policy forum in Wales saying, 'There is little point having devolution if all we are going to do is have expensive photocopies of the policies that come out of Westminster'.[17]

There must be a careful balance. When Rhodri Morgan became First Minister he quickly and rightly sought to move away from the control-freakery style of his predecessor Alun Michael and New Labour colleagues in Westminster, by making more Welsh-based decisions. However, in creating 'clear-red-water' policies, his administration has often gone a step too far and shunned ones that have worked well over the border. While it is important to find Welsh solutions to Welsh problems, it is not in the interest of Wales to seek to be different for the sake of it – at the expense of better public services. It is a point that has been recognized on more than one occasion by Welsh Labour MPs in Westminster. There is frustration over the manner in which Labour in the Assembly has ignored the greater emphasis on choice in public services in England and the benefits they would bring to Welsh health and education. Ideological barriers have given the government fewer tools at their disposal.

There are times when Wales should tread a different path from England and times when lessons can be learned from other countries in the UK and the rest of the world. Welsh Conservative policy must be pragmatic and not driven by dogma. People in England have benefited from choice and diversity in their public services. The Welsh people want high-quality schools and hospitals; they are not preoccupied with the ideological debate. Moreover, it will be to the advantage of the Welsh people if the Assembly government moves away from headline-grabbing gimmicks. Several of the Labour 'top ten pledges' in their 2003 manifesto, have proved to be empty promises and have been quietly dropped, most recently the promise of free home care for the disabled. Effective policies will be judged on their long-term difference to Welsh quality of life.

I believe one way to make the Assembly a success is to deliver true devolution to the people of Wales. This would involve a shift away from the centralist grip of government and developing local solutions. The concept of 'civic Conservatism' is something that Welsh Conservatives have been promoting for sometime; moving power away from government to Welsh people themselves in their communities. This would involve more power being given to community councils, local hospitals and local schools.

The failure of Welsh Labour to inspire the Welsh people throws down the gauntlet to other parties to come up with a non-Labour alternative government. It is only the Welsh Conservatives who are shaping up to the challenge. Part of the reason for sceptical opinion of the Assembly is that even though hospital waiting lists are unacceptably long and council tax has gone through the roof, there is no real prospect of a change of government. This appearance of a 'one-party state' leads to stale politics and, undoubtedly, adds to voter apathy. Frequently, criticism is directed at the institution when the real frustration lies with Government decisions. Only by offering a true alternative will the Assembly thrive and only then will the people of Wales be proud and have confidence in their Assembly. Welsh Conservatives are serious about change and Labour dominance is being challenged.

Conclusion

Welsh Conservatives have come a long way since the advent of devolution – indeed they have flourished under the devolved settlement. Instead of it signalling the death knell, Welsh Conservatives are not only alive and kicking but arguably the main beneficiaries of the Assembly. The party is widely recognized to be the hardest-working group and Labour's most formidable opponents. In 1997, Conservatives had no MPs in Wales and fewer than 40 councillors. In 2006, we have 11 AMs, three MPs and 110 councillors. The statistics speak for themselves.

In the very first days of the Assembly, Rhodri Morgan said: 'Our task is clear: to prove the battle for devolution was worth it by making a real difference to the lives of the people of Wales.'[18] Seven years later and there remains a great deal of work to be done. As long as Welsh Conservatives remain true to Welsh values of community they will go from strength to strength. This will certainly mean looking at new solutions to tackle community problems. I strongly believe that making it easier for social enterprises and voluntary organizations to provide solutions to problems is part of the agenda which Conservatives must espouse. Thus we have voluntary organizations helping with things as diverse as recycling, homelessness, drug and alcohol abuse and helping young people into work. These organizations should be helped not hindered by simplifying planning and licensing procedures and providing incentives where they are able, as is most often the case, to make a real difference in their communities. Additionally, we must recognize the importance attached by local communities to their community hospitals, their post offices, their local police station and their local schools. Increasing centralization and attempts at cost cutting by opting for a 'big is beautiful' solution are both unpopular and doomed to failure. This is not the Conservative way and Conservative policy has accordingly favoured small and local solutions and the preservation and enhancement of local institutions. Localism and devolution is the best way forward for Welsh Conservatives and for Wales.

NOTES

[1] Labour Party Manifesto, 1997.

[2] Liberal Democrat Manifesto, 1997; Plaid Cymru Manifesto, 1997.

[3] Conservative Party Manifesto, 1997.

[4] 'Tories hit at Welsh assembly costs', *Financial Times*, 20 May 1998.

[5] 'Oh No', *Financial Times*, 18 September 1997.

[6] 'Davies warns of "last chance"', *Guardian*, 11 September 1997.

[7] 'Welsh Labour MPs told to toe line', *Guardian*, 16 May 1997; 'Welsh Devolution: Poll blow to Yes Camp', *Guardian*, 16 September 1997.

[8] 'Devolution "A dynamic, settled process"?', *Monitoring the Assembly July to December 1999*, Institute of Welsh Affairs, December 1999.

[9] National Assembly for Wales, *The Official Record*, 9 February 2000.

[10] 'CBI Wales attacks assembly', *Financial Times*, 4 December 1997.

[11] 'Devolution has more than doubled cost of administering government in Wales', *Financial Times*, 8 March 2002.

[12] *Ibid.*

[13] 'Nine quangos face devolution axe', *Guardian*, 22 July 1997.

[14] WAQ44496.

[15] *Report of the Richard Commission*, 2004, 44–45.

[16] 'Hague warns Welsh against "costly error"', *The Times*, 9 September 1997.

[17] 'Bourne wants a think tank with deep blue Welsh water', *Western Mail*, 7 October 2003.

THE IDIOMS OF RACE: THE 'RACIST NATIONALIST' IN WALES AS BOGEYMAN

Simon Brooks

In early twenty-first-century Wales no idiom was used more often of political dissent than that of 'racism', and nowhere more so than in the ritualized condemnations of language campaigners that characterized the period. This is odd, for we have come to think in Britain of anti-racism as synonymous with the protection of ethnic and cultural minorities. In Wales, however, the world was turned upside down, and it was a minority that was attacked in the name of 'anti-racism' for supposed intolerance, xenophobia and ethnic hatred. It is no coincidence that these attacks dovetail into the period that began with the first National Assembly elections in 1999, when Plaid Cymru won 17 seats and seemed set to challenge Labour hegemony in Wales and subsided in 2003, when the nationalists lost five of their seats and that threat receded. It is the contention of this chapter that many of the attacks on language activism in 1999–2003 were manufactured, and that their true purpose was to smear activists in the hope that this would damage Plaid Cymru. Centre stage was the 'Seimon Glyn affair', a public row about the supposed relationship between language, racism and nationalism which began with a low-key radio interview given by a Plaid Cymru Gwynedd councillor in January 2001, and then dominated political debate in Wales for the following two years. This chapter will explore the discourse and idioms that enabled the Labour Party, and its allies in the tabloid media, to create in this period a bogeyman, that of the 'racist nationalist', a figure that featured more prominently perhaps in the imagination than it did in reality.

In the lexicography of duplicitous political terms, wrote academic Patrick McGuinness in 2003, Wales has the 'volatile newspeak of *race, racism* and their cognates [. . .] a vast and daily-renewed living archive [. . .] a kind of discursive free-for-all'. These idioms aim to construct a 'race-language link' that will reach 'hysterical proportions' being 'played again and again'.[1] Yet, as McGuinness notes, the emergence of the 'language-race' idiom is not a consequence of minority-language activism. Welsh-language activists are subjects in this discourse, not its makers; although they stand condemned by it.

I came across these idioms when, between 2001 and 2003, I led Cymuned, the pressure group founded in the wake of the Seimon Glyn affair, to defend him from accusations of 'racism', and to campaign for Welsh-speaking communities. 'Racism' proved to be infectious: before long I was being told by politicians and the media that Cymuned too had caught the bug. This raised for me an important question: how was it that the rhetoric of anti-racism came to be used in Wales to demonize and vilify campaigners for a minority language?

The immediate excuse for linking language activism with racism is that activists have concerned themselves with population movement into Welsh-speaking communities, and that such concerns can be made, through the prism of racialized idioms, to seem similar to the Far Right's obsession with immigration. This ignores that in-migration into minority language communities, and the language change it effects, are different from the impact of immigration by marginalized peoples on strong State cultures with all the power to acculturate those who move in. Because language is a social phenomenon, it is essential that communities exist where Welsh is the normative language of mundane, everyday communication. Such communities are not cover for the discredited dream of a racially-pure or culturally-homogenous organic community. They are the empirically proven base for the survival of a minority language.[2]

As the vast majority of in-migrants to Welsh-speaking communities are from England, it became possible for political debate about migration and the Welsh language to be charged with the idioms of race. For those opposed to language activism, protecting Welsh-speaking communities became synonymous with anti-English sentiment: a view not shared by language activists themselves. In truth, there is no evidence that either the English or the English language face nationalist-led discrimination in Wales. The English are, after all, the dominant majority within the British State, and English is the language of the State, which also happens to be the language of the new globalized world order. Such things confer power. Statistically, the English-born are proportionally over-represented in Wales in the upper echelons of the job market.[3] They are well represented in civil society and representative democracy, including in the Welsh Assembly and Government.[4] Furthermore, they are active in Welsh nationalism: at senior levels in Plaid Cymru and in language activism.[5] It is hard to think of the English as an 'excluded minority' in the same way as Afro-Caribbeans or Asians. The English in Wales are what has been called by theorists a 'dominant minority [. . .] a different thing from the poor and frequently despised immigrants who have figured more often in modern Welsh history'.[6]

This is not to deny that racism exists in Welsh communities. Racism exists in all communities, and Wales is no exception. Some English people have faced racism and prejudice for no other reason than their nationality. This is deplorable. There have been occasional physical attacks on those taken to be English.[7] Welsh-language culture can be ethnocentric.[8] However, there is no evidence of any correlation between language activism and racism. No Welsh-language activist has ever been charged, cautioned or convicted for any racial, or racially-aggravated, offence. Because anti-English racism exists in Wales, it does not follow that nationalists and language activists are responsible for it.

What then gave rise to the idiom of the 'racist-nationalist' bogeyman? It did not of course arrive in the Wales of 1999 from nowhere. Similar discourses have been circulating in Wales for the better part of the twentieth century. One writer saw connections between the idiom and attacks on the language in the 1847 Blue Books: both attempted to humiliate Welsh-speakers with the stigma of moral failing.[9] The 'racist-nationalist' discourse could even be said to date back to the eighteenth century and the Enlightenment, when minority languages and nations were denied 'rationality' and reduced to the status of emotional patois. It is from the Enlightenment that the democratic, internationalist, socialist ideal of equality through a common citizenship based on a common language and common culture springs. According to this discourse, much beloved by elements of the Labour party in Wales, a language like Welsh, spoken by a minority, is elitist, divisive, exclusive.[10] It is 'ethnic' rather than 'civic', and can thus, by symbiosis, become racist and fascist.

The 'racist-nationalist' bogeyman has its more recent historical roots, however, as an idiom used against Plaid Cymru since its foundation in 1925. That idiom is one of fascism. It talks of Plaid Cymru, in the words of one 1942 essayist, wanting to create 'a fascist, totalitarian' Wales.[11] Part of this can be put down to the tensions of the Second World War, during which Plaid Cymru maintained a position of neutrality. Yet the political longevity of the claim suggests that other factors may be at work. Labour MPs in post-war Wales talked of links between Nazism and Plaid Cymru, while the Nazi metaphor was used about Welsh language 'purity' too.[12] Other times of tension for the Unionist Labour tradition also saw the Nazi metaphor employed, in particular during the crucial years following the election in 1966 of Gwynfor Evans as Plaid Cymru's first MP, when it appeared that Labour was on the back foot,[13] and before the 1979 devolution referendum, when many Labour MPs rebelled against the party line to campaign for a No Vote. 'There is no magic superiority of one language over the others though Nazi and German academics preached this dangerous doctrine', mused Pontypool MP Leo Abse six months before the referendum, '[. . .] the Welsh language fanatic believes the language speaks through him, [. . .] and spurred by his arrogance he has already made dangerous gains.'[14]

It is significant therefore that 1999–2003 saw increased prominence given to attacks on Saunders Lewis as a racist, fascist, English-hater and Nazi.[15] It shows that the 'language-race' idioms of twenty-first-century Wales were understood by Labour as part of a narrative going back to the birth of Plaid Cymru. In a 2002 debate in the House of Commons on 'racism' in Welsh politics, the history of language activism was condensed to a simple archaeology: there was a link between 'anti-semite' Saunders

Lewis who 'had sympathies for Mussolini, Franco and Hitler', and 'the racism and xenophobia inherent' in modern day Plaid Cymru, and amongst 'language extremists'.[16]

Concluding that there is no evidence that Plaid Cymru was ever a Fascist party, Richard Wyn Jones explores some of the rhetorical devices exploited to link Welsh nationalism with Nazism.[17] Articles which give intellectual credence to the accusation are based upon dubious scholarship. Opinion-formers of the day, in particular the tabloid press and leading Labour politicians, make sweeping statements, without particular reference to the facts. Statements by leading nationalists, including Saunders Lewis, opposing Fascism are simply edited out of the archive.[18] The existence of real Fascist sympathy in Wales – in 1931, for example, Oswald Mosley's New Party gained more than 10,000 votes in Merthyr – is ignored: it is replaced by rhetorical hysteria about a party with no Fascist leanings at all.

Interestingly, these idioms of deceit all have their direct rhetorical parallels in the 'language-race' synopses of the early twenty-first century, and the Seimon Glyn affair. Richard Wyn Jones concludes that the Plaid Cymru-Fascist link is living proof that a Big Lie can be accepted as Truth when it is repeated, and not challenged. 'These accusations represent an attempt to exile Plaid Cymru from the midst of political discussion in Wales – to expel it from the sphere of "the acceptable".'[19]

During the second half of the twentieth century, the idiom of 'nationalism is fascism' gradually gave way to a new formula: 'nationalism is racism'. As 'racism' began to displace 'fascism' as the main threat to democracy and equality in post-war Britain, new accusations were made by those who wished to stigmatize the Welsh-speaking minority. 'Racism', 'apartheid', 'ethnic cleansing', and other expressions of ethnic intolerance and absolutism, were emptied of their real historical meaning and applied to Welsh nationalism. They were employed without regard for what they addressed, and acted as synonyms that slid into each other. The rule of thumb seems to be that these idioms are lifted from various ethnically-based crises of the day. In the 1980s, one has references to apartheid.[20] In the early and mid 1990s, there is 'ethnic cleansing', the conflict in the former Yugoslavia, and 'the

Balkanization of Britain'.[21] However they are all played against a
constant backdrop, that of the idioms of race.

From the late 1960s these idioms abounded in Wales and were
transported into language politics largely because of the new
prominence of race in British political life. Enoch Powell's
notorious 'rivers of blood' speech in 1968 provided an early
opportunity for 'racialization' in Wales with warnings that anti-
black prejudice could lead to racism between the English and the
Welsh.[22] However, it is the Race Relations Act 1976, establishing
the Commission for Racial Equality (CRE) and a framework for
advising on 'settling disputes of language discrimination', which
allows the discourse to take off.[23]

Parallels with the wider British immigration debate mean that
discussion of in-migration in rural Wales is invariably described as
racist. Idioms from this wider debate are present when, in 1976, a
Gwynedd County Council committee refused on principle to
discuss a Cymdeithas yr Iaith Gymraeg (Welsh Language Society)
policy document which called for limits on 'English' in-migration;
one councillor calling it 'racialist filth'.[24] A 1982 Gwynedd County
Council discussion document expressing concern about the effect
of in-migration on education caused a similar furore.[25] The late
1980s, which saw a boom in the housing market and increased
rates of in-migration into rural Wales, sees the use of these idioms
peak. Newspapers are full of letters belying Welsh-language
'racism'. Columnists like the *Daily Post*'s Ivor Wynne Jones feed
the frenzy with hyperbole, talking of 'an isolationist Gwynedd in
search of its lost master race', a 'final solution', and a 'bastard'
politics 'with all the attributes of Adolf Hitler or Idi Amin'.[26]
Increasingly, the CRE becomes involved, racializing the language
debate on planning and housing, both at a rhetorical (a Bala farmer
attracted censure after demanding to sell his farm to local buyers,
for example) and policy level: Ceredigion District Council faced
the threat of legal action in 1995 after a proposed housing policy
was branded as racist.[27] The common denominator of these
accusations of 'racism' was their use as a 'catch-all', to
delegitimize expressions of linguistic dissent which differed in
some way from a British cultural-political norm, and in particular

those forms of dissent that touched on the issue of population movement within the British Isles.

The politics of race was also used to undermine the role of Welsh in civil society. Arguing that Welsh language requirements in employment could constitute indirect discrimination against the English as an ethnic group, a string of cases was heard in industrial tribunals. In 1979, a case was brought against Dyfed Area Health Authority for requiring a speech therapist working with Welsh-speaking children in Ceredigion to be able to speak Welsh.[28] Although the applicant lost, a similar case brought in 1985 by the CRE on behalf of two women against Gwynedd County Council for requiring care home workers to be able to speak Welsh was successful. Later reversed on appeal, the judgement provoked considerable anguish among nationalists. The Plaid Cymru MP for Caernarfon, Dafydd Wigley, accused the CRE of 'vindictiveness and a vendetta [. . .] to put the boot into the Welsh language', and sought a change in the law.[29] Over the next decade the CRE would attach itself to a number of similar cases, in particular in 1995 when it threatened legal action over the use of Welsh as the language of internal administration in the new Caernarfonshire and Merionethshire (later Gwynedd) County Council.[30]

The key to the CRE's ideological position is perhaps best explained by its reference to Welsh in 1985 as a 'community language'.[31] Welsh was not the language of the State: its proposed use as condition of employment or residence would discriminate against a common British citizenship based on the English language. Such an analysis would lead language activists during the Seimon Glyn affair to accuse the CRE of 'institutionalised racism' against the Welsh-speaking Welsh, and of being a prop of British State nationalism.[32] Certainly, the CRE's historical antipathy towards language activism was an important bulwark of the 'language-race' discourse, and gave institutional credence to the idea that language activists were racists.

The idea that language activism was in some way connected to racism was thus already well established as a propaganda tool by 1999, and the onset of devolution. The creation of 'racist nationalism' in early twenty-first-century Wales is in many ways merely an extension of this late twentieth-century discourse. But the first Assembly term of 1999-2003 offered the idiom a new political context. This was a period when Welsh nationalism appeared to be a threat to Unionist dominance in Wales in a way that it was not during the pre-devolution years. As the need to attack Plaid Cymru became a strategic priority for the Labour Party, the 'idiom of race' mutated, and the breadth and depth of attacks on nationalist 'racism' became wider and deeper. They also increased considerably in volume, becoming a daily ritual by 2001 and 2002.

A central feature of this new mutated 'language-race' idiom was that it was independent of events. Much journalism in 1999-2003, particularly in English, took it as read that it was language activists who were responsible for pushing the 'language-race' problem to the top of the post-devolution political agenda. They assumed that activists had employed with intent a series of racialized idioms, thus provoking justified condemnation. Yet the reality was that nationalist discourse was being racialized by others for political reasons, using a variety of discursive tactics to create an uncomplimentary image. This was understood by many Welsh speakers. Cymuned was initially so successful, drawing 500 people to its inaugural meeting in North Wales in July 2001, not because of English in-migration but because Welsh-speakers felt they were being demonized in the press, and tarred with a brush – that of racism – which they did not deserve.

The tabloid press had been plying a 'racist-nationalist' narrative to attack Welsh nationalism for well over a year before the Seimon Glyn affair, the first emergence of any 'evidence' to support the racism thesis. In the first instalment in July 1999 of his soon-to-be infamous weekly column, *Welsh Mirror* journalist Paul Starling wrote that 'narrow nationalisms' let loose 'mayhem and murder'.[33] He continued in a similar vein for the rest of 1999 and 2000, warning of 'racist nationalism' and 'ethnic-and-language control', while a front page article in August 2000 attacked Welsh-language activists as fascists.[34] Plaid Cymru members had been condemned as 'daft racists and xenophobes' months before the Seimon Glyn affair.[35] With Welsh-language activism at a low ebb during the Welsh Assembly's initial honeymoon period, these attacks bore no relation to any events-driven reality.

The Labour party too had been promoting the 'racist-nationalist' agenda since 1999 with little regard to a lack of evidence. As early as September 1999, the Assembly's First Secretary, Alun Michael, wrote of 'the dangers and the destructiveness of narrow nationalism' that had blighted Europe.[36] There seems at some point following the first Assembly Elections to have been a strategic decision by Labour to play the 'Orange card' of Welsh politics, that of presenting Welsh-language 'extremism' as a threat to the English-speaking population. In Labour's Welsh headquarters, plans were laid that would facilitate the seeking and exposing of 'extremist' statements made by nationalists and language activists. A Welsh-speaking media officer was employed to monitor the hitherto ignored Welsh-language press, and to release transcripts of monitored material, in both English and Welsh, to tabloid newspapers, in particular the *Welsh Mirror*.

The Seimon Glyn affair showed Labour's political strategy to racialize Welsh politics at work. On 17 January, 2001, a Gwynedd county councillor, Seimon Glyn, was a guest on a BBC Radio Wales phone-in programme. During chat with the programme's presenter, Seimon Glyn made a number of controversial and contested statements about in-migration. These statements included: 'Once you have more than 50% of anybody living in a community who speaks a foreign language then you lose your indigenous tongue almost immediately and this is what's happening in our rural villages' and 'We're faced with a situation now where we are getting tidal waves of migration, inward migration into our rural areas from England and these people are coming to live, to establish themselves here and to influence our communities and our culture with their own. [. . .] Now if they were coming here under strict monitoring and control and if, for example, they were made aware of you know the different cultural aspects of these areas and made to or be persuaded to learn Welsh and to integrate smoothly into our communities there wouldn't be a problem.'[37]

These statements attracted a range of varying interpretations. They clearly belong to the genre, common since the late 1960s, of bemoaning the linguistic effects of in-migration from England on Welsh-speaking communities in rural Wales. But were they racist?

Did they seek to denigrate 'English' residents 'in Wales'? References to 'a foreign language [. . .] in our rural villages', 'inward migration into our rural areas' and 'the different cultural aspects of these areas' would suggest that Seimon Glyn is talking about migration to Welsh-speaking communities rather than to Wales as a whole: which in turn would suggest a linguistic, rather than 'racial', rationale to the interview. A Bangor sociologist, Delyth Morris, concluded that Seimon Glyn hadn't been 'racist according to the provisions of the Race Relations Act' as he hadn't 'directly addressed any individual subject in ethnic or racist terms'.[38] North Wales Chief Constable Richard Brunstrom later came to the same conclusion: 'there is no evidence you intended to create racial hatred'.[39]

This, however, was not the view of the Labour Party in Wales, which saw a made-to-fit example that would prove the existence of the 'racist-nationalist' bogeyman. Yet the transformation of Seimon Glyn's words from ephemeral statement to political narrative was of Labour's own making. A Labour press release providing a transcript of the interview was distributed. Next day, in a front page story, 'Voice of Hate', the *Welsh Mirror* eliminated any possible nuances and condensed his message into sound-bite format for popular consumption. As Seimon Glyn had made no direct references to 'the English' in his interview, these were added by the *Welsh Mirror* in its reportage: 'English residents in Wales should be monitored' and 'English is a foreign language in Wales'.[40]

Subsequent Labour condemnation of Seimon Glyn solidified these idioms of 'racist nationalism'. An Early Day Motion tabled in the House of Commons by a Welsh Labour MP quoted Seimon Glyn, rather creatively, as 'accusing English residents of "invading" Wales'.[41] The Secretary of State for Wales, Paul Murphy, claimed that Seimon Glyn had said that 'incomers from Chester' should be monitored and controlled.[42] In an article in the *Welsh Mirror*, the Prime Minister, Tony Blair, expressed his 'hate' for 'the intolerance within Plaid Cymru with their attacks on English as a foreign language and their demands that English incomers should be strictly monitored.'[43] By such rhetorical devices, the belief that Seimon Glyn had said that English people coming to Wales should be 'monitored' and that English is a 'foreign' language in Wales became entrenched in the public mind as direct quotations, and as part of a wider xenophobia.[44]

After the first few months of the Seimon Glyn affair, it became necessary for the Labour party, and the tabloid press, to use such devices to create more 'racist nationalists', to keep the 'race-language' narrative going. This was achieved by extensive 'trawling' for evidence, cherry-picking and selective editing. If a text was open to both a racialized and non-racialized reading, only the racialized reading would be used, and the non-racialized version would be ignored.

Obscure comments made by Gwilym ab Ioan, a member of Plaid Cymru's National Executive, about English 'oddballs, social misfits and society dropouts' were extracted from the political underworld of an internet forum.[45] A Plaid Cymru councillor was condemned for condemning British imperialism, because in doing so he had accused the 'English' of having 'raped [. . .] every country that they've been in'.[46] Leanne Wood, a Plaid Cymru General Election candidate, became involved in a 'campaign race row' and was accused of 'whipping up hatred' after calling Labour a 'British nationalist' party.[47] There were attempts to smear Plaid Cymru MEPs for alleged 'links to a European Separatist Party which supports Nazi collaborators'.[48] Eifion Lloyd Jones was identified as a 'former Plaid Cymru General Election candidate' after expressing controversial and allegedly racist views on Welsh-medium education.[49] Heini Gruffudd, a language activist in Swansea, was condemned for racism on account of the phrase '*twll tin pob Sais*' contained in a book for Welsh learners.[50] At the height of the 'race row', said one commentator, racism was being used 'in politics and media for everything from supporting the Welsh football team to the Welsh Language Act, from advertising jobs that require fluency in Welsh to S4C's lack of subtitles'.[51]

In all this there was one case of a racist metaphor. John Elfed Jones, a former head of the Welsh Language Board, had used the words 'feet' (*traed*) and 'mouths' (*genau*), to argue that those who 'move in' ('*troedio i mewn*') to Welsh-speaking communities change that which comes from the 'mouths' of men, namely language.[52] In one sense, a non-racial play on words, '*clwy'r traed a'r genau'* is also a diseased metaphor: foot-and-mouth disease. As the only case of a Welsh-language activist employing terminology that can be read at the level of biological racism, his choice of language is to be deeply regretted.

Other examples of 'racist nationalism' required tampering, curious translation and loaded commentary. In another 2001 Welsh-language article, journalist Beca Brown had claimed that she, as a member of a minority, harboured 'racist' feelings towards a 'colonial' majority. Such feelings were unacceptable and had to be challenged: 'racism breeds bullying – and we have to release ourselves from this terrible cycle.'[53] Using a doctored translation of her text – translating *cenedl* ('nation') as race – the tabloid *Wales on Sunday* reprinted much of the article, but chose to edit out the final paragraph that condemned such 'racism' as bullying.[54] This allowed her to be branded as a racist. 'Disgraceful!' remarked rebel Labour MP, Paul Flynn, who condemned his own party for a 'witch-hunt' against language activists: 'She bravely attacked her own prejudices and warned that racism was bullying. A Welsh journalist with a brain – and one that works too!'[55]

Others fell victim to this strategy of selective mistranslation.[56] Indeed a key part of the 'racist-nationalist' strategy was to use doctored articles 'translated' from Welsh. Politicians and opinion formers who could not read Welsh would have no way of checking either the accuracy of quotes or the context in which they were made. Left unchallenged, of course, such 'racist' comments, which in many cases had never been said, entered Welsh public life as fact.

Another part of the discourse was to close down any chance for Welsh-language activists to present their own case in their own words. This denied them the chance to speak without being mediated through the prism of racist narrative. Official complaints were lodged when language activists appeared on the BBC and calls were made in the Commons to withdraw public subsidy from *Barn*, a current affairs magazine that had supported language activism.[57] The cause célèbre was an attempt in May 2001 by Labour to censor the evidence of a nationalist academic, Dafydd Glyn Jones, to an Assembly committee. He claimed that the English would be 'hopping mad' at the development of Welsh-medium higher education. If his paper were considered, said Labour AM, Huw Lewis, Assembly committees might have to consider 'outrageous, sexist, xenophobic, racist, inflammatory, even illegal statements in the future'.[58] The Labour Education Minister, Jane Davidson, suggested that evidence might be vetted beforehand by the Assembly Secretariat so that potentially offensive material could be removed. The idea was rejected following legal advice that this would contravene the European Convention on Human Rights. Yet the approach shows the Labour mindset. The aim seems to have been not just to rebut language arguments, but by using the 'race-language' discourse, to delegitimize them. This was well understood at the time: 48 Welsh-speaking academics in the University of Wales signed a declaration 'expressing disbelief at the sinister and irresponsible way that a debate about the rights of the Welsh-speaking community has, once again, been distorted and falsely turned into a matter of "racism" and "xenophobia".'[59]

Similar strategies of delegitimization were carried forward in other ways. Having demarcated a racialized reading of comments, 'racist nationalists' could then be accused of intent to incite racial hatred.[60] Many Labour AMs and MPs refused to be lobbied by Cymuned; some argued that it was a racist organisation.[61] Two Labour AMs threatened to refer evidence placed before the Assembly by Cymuned to the Home Office, with a view to seeking prosecution 'under new race laws'.[62] Guidelines that allowed people to self-define racial harassment enabled those opposed to language activism to file subjective complaints that forced the removal of much Cymuned material in Gwynedd from public display.[63] These referrals on 'suspicion' of race hate offences were a crucial part of the 'racist-nationalist' strategy because they kept alive in voters' minds, on the basis that there is no smoke without fire, the inherent 'racism' of minority rights activists. They appeared to give the concept of 'racist nationalism' an 'objective' and quasi-legal base. Inevitably, the result of such pressure was to persuade many not to challenge the 'racist-nationalist' discourse. 'Put together British censorship, the self-censorship of the Welsh-speaking Welsh and the response of a member of a Race Relations Board,' remarked one columnist, 'and we have the strange situation where a man could be arrested for discussing the death of the Welsh language.'[64]

A key ally of Labour in the creation of the idioms of 'racist nationalism' was the tabloid *Welsh Mirror*, which had launched a 'regional' edition following devolution with a strongly anti-nationalist editorial line. 'Wales' most popular newspaper has raised nat-bashing to levels which border on self-parody', wrote Richard Wyn Jones in 2002, 'every time I read Paul Starling, I am reminded of *Private Eye*'s spoof headline for the *Daily Mail* about Labour planning to kill the first-born.'[65] Nicknamed the 'anti-Welsh Mirror', the paper pursued Welsh-language activists in a campaign of vilification comparable to the 'loony left' journalism of the 1980s, when minority rights activists were targeted by the Thatcherite *Sun*.[66] The *Welsh Mirror* compared nationalism and language activism with Ireland, Yugoslavia, apartheid and ethnic cleansing.[67] Such activism celebrated 'soil, blood, language and race'; it was 'fascism', while Plaid Cymru's claim to be both socialist and nationalist harked back to National Socialism.[68] There was reference to a new category of terrorism, 'racist terrorists', and an anonymous communication from 'a man convinced that language extremism, aimed at his family, led to the premature death of his father'.[69] Language activists were invariably 'language loonies' or 'language nutters', and readers were urged to 'drive out these people from our midst.'[70] Attacks on Welsh-language activism soon spilt over into attacks on the Welsh language itself. Welsh was labelled 'a secret code' and Welsh-language articles were published 'under the cover of the Welsh language'.[71] The Eisteddfod became the 'festival of fear and hatred'.[72] Pejorative terms for the language, its speakers and activists become common currency in social discourse, and spread beyond their tabloid roots. They began to impact on the underlying editorial assumptions of more neutral and liberal media. In 2003, even an academic like Charlotte Williams could refer to Welsh-language activists as 'the tribes' and belittle campaigners as 'Knights of Glyndŵr'.[73]

Several commentators have noted the similarity between the 'racist-nationalist' discourse and 'minority-bashing' campaigns. 'It uses the key ingredients', said Patrick McGuinness, 'the fostering of resentment, the myth of the "enemy within" [. . .], the transformation of a minority activist into an "extremist", and the ensuing identification of alleged "extremists" with the entire culture.'[74] Elements were borrowed from homophobic discourse: in the *Welsh Mirror*'s description of Plaid Cymru chief executive, Dafydd Trystan, as a 'raving nationalist', for example.[75] The idea of Welsh-speakers as 'an enemy within' was similar in its way, said Tim Saunders, to anti-Semitism: 'Those of us who speak Welsh are a double danger. At the same time we are primitive creatures who are hostile to everyone who isn't similar to us, but we are also sophisticated impostors who are taking over all of society through guile and conspiracy.'[76] While poor rural Welsh-speakers were seen as rednecks, 'racist' against outsiders; wealthy urban Welsh-speakers, perhaps working for the BBC or S4C, were trading on their 'racial' background to gain unfair advantage.

The 'Welsh language elite', said Paul Starling, was an 'army of gin-slingers', a 'linguistic freemasonry'.[77] The 'crachach' was 'divisive, racist, dangerous, selfish'.[78] Certainly, such attacks on a moneyed middle class from a minority background would fit the 'anti-Semitic' mould. It was, said McGuinness, an 'internally-directed xenophobia', one which played upon faked class war rhetoric.[79] The *Welsh Mirror* developed a line in cartoons the most notorious of which portrayed an object marked 'Welsh language' being rammed down a sweating man's throat, his eyes lit up by fear.[80] These too were seen as pejorative.

We have thus identified the initial strategies that enabled the construction of a 'racist-nationalist' discourse: the manufacture by discursive shape-shifting of a prima facie case of racism; in short, the collation of 'primary evidence' to suit a predetermined thesis. The mass media then picks up the baton and subjects this 'evidence' to commentary and analysis that attempts to 'solidify' and emphasize 'racist' meaning. It does this by hyperbole, exaggeration and distortion. Above all, there is the sheer volume of the reportage: any idiom used this often, apparently on the record and without rebuttal, must surely be true. This journalism is the 'first draft of history'; it is the initial secondary source on which subsequent commentaries will be built.

The crucial stage, however, is the validation of this secondary material; for the tabloid newspaper does not, of itself, constitute a medium of record. Given the absence in Wales of intelligent print media, this institutionalization of the 'racist-nationalist' idiom takes place in academia, in the disciplines of political science and sociology. It is particularly noticeable that many of these studies draw upon newspaper reports, not to analyse a manufactured idiom, but as neutral reflection of public opinion. Part of the problem, of course, is that while secondary source material exists in English, most of the primary source material is in Welsh. As English is the language of nearly all academic writing in the social sciences, and as many academics and commentators cannot read Welsh, the Welsh-language primary sources are ignored. Academic analysis is thus based on the filtered commentaries of newspapers in English, and upon the work of other academics, but only those who write in English. Welsh-language secondary sources are neither read nor referenced. Once academic articles exist that offer 'footnoted' proof of racism, the 'racist-nationalist' discourse is solidified as history. This is the truest moment of its creation. The discourse has now become empirical reality; and can be repeated, *ad infinitum*, as fact.

Examples can be given of this process at work. In a series of articles on racism, language and Welsh nationalism in the 1990s, non-Welsh-speaking sociologists made a series of claims about Welsh-language activism and nationalism that might be said to fit into the 'racist-nationalist' discourse.[81] Rarely, if at all, do these articles footnote a Welsh-language source. They do, however, make liberal use of English-language newspapers; accessing, apparently at random, the idioms of 'racist nationalism' in articles and letters. More recently a key player in the academic canonization of the 'racist nationalism' myth has been Charlotte Williams. In *Planet*, she repeated the erroneous suggestion, lifted from the *Wales on Sunday*, that Beca Brown hates the English 'as a race': an example of the 'racist-nationalist' idiom following through, all the way from doctored translation via tabloid *exposé* to academic 'fact'.[82] In *A Tolerant Nation?* – a seminal academic study of multiculturalism and race relations in Wales – she accuses Seimon Glyn of 'racist terminology', claims that Cymuned wants 'restricted areas in Wales earmarked for Welsh speakers' and states that Cymdeithas yr Iaith 'frequently used the term "white settlers" to describe English incomers, explicitly evoking racist categories'.[83] These are tabloidized claims at best, questionable in their accuracy, marked by loaded use of adjective and characterized by journalistic hyperbole. By such means, however, the 'racist-nationalist' myth can be disseminated in academia worldwide, to be referenced by international scholars as empirical evidence of Welsh racism.

The 'racist-nationalist' myth is institutionalized in the British and international mass media too. Its entry into British discourse via London newspapers has a long history in Wales.[84] Such a discourse makes claims about Welsh racism and xenophobia, often by those with xenophobic tendencies themselves: 'The outsiders are not criminals, layabouts or scroungers. [. . .] They are not gypsies', wrote Robert Kilroy Silk in the *Express*, 'the crime the outsiders have committed is to be English.'[85] Similar idioms were replayed in the wake of the Seimon Glyn affair: the *Observer*, for example, linking anti-Asian racism in the police force with supposed anti-black racism among Welsh-speaking farmers.[86] The idiom also penetrates media at the highest level, in texts involved in international representations of Wales. Global brand travel guide *Lonely Planet* reports in its 2004 Wales edition, without any supporting evidence whatsoever, that 'young nationalists have recently been targeting non-Welsh speakers and the tiny minority population of blacks and Asians.'[87] Thus misinformation becomes urban myth becomes fact. In an age of online news and Google searches, these idioms of 'racist nationalism' can be spread in supranational cyberspace: a bone of contention among those responsible for the Plaid Cymru entry on the Web-based 'encyclopaedia' Wikipedia, for example, is the Seimon Glyn affair.[88]

Here, then, we see the disciplines of journalism, travel writing and social science engage in the collection of a series of motley and unconnected statements in order to create a mythical discourse about Welsh language activists, and nationalists, that does not, in reality, exist. Such writing about Wales is similar in many ways to how other minority or 'exotic' communities have been historically imagined. Edward Said's depiction in *Orientalism* of the Western World creating a racialized discourse about the Middle East is not wholly dissimilar to the process by which this racialized discourse of Welsh-speaking Wales is put together.[89] 'Their source of evidence [. . .] is a discourse on a discourse!' exclaimed Glyn Williams about one academic article that discussed 'race' and the Welsh-language community.[90] This secondary sourced 'orientalized' writing imagines, concocts and manufactures Welsh-language activism in a way that enables the production of yet more writing in the same vein. It is part of a self-referring circle. It is not a discussion of the Welsh-language community, but a discussion of a representation of the Welsh-language community.

Untrue accusations made by international brands such as *Lonely Planet* show the rhetorical need for the idioms of 'racist nationalism' to make the crossover from 'anti-English racism' to racism against blacks and Asians. In a way, this represents the 'globalization' of the 'racist-nationalist' bogeyman; from a rather parochial discrimination against a fellow 'European' ethnic group to one which can be understood anywhere on the planet. The 'mark up' gained by this was understood by those manufacturing the discourse in Wales. In essence, it 'sexed up' the 'racism'. It made credible claims that language activists were 'as bad as the far right'.[91] It gave credence too to a Labour strategy so simple that it could be expressed as an equation: 'BNP = Cymuned = Plaid Cymru'.[92] White members of the Labour Party could therefore use ethnic minorities to head up the attack on Welsh-language activists, thus casting the 'language-race' dispute in terms of facing down white racism.[93] Under Secretary of State for Wales, Don Touhig suggested that Welsh-language activists would benefit from reflecting on the legacy of Martin Luther King.[94] Claims by Dafydd Iwan of a racist 'white flight' from multicultural urban conurbations to rural Wales also led to accusations of causing offence to ethnic minorities.[95]

However, this suggestion of points of tension between Welsh-language activism and multiculturalism was not without foundation. Those who believed in the existence of a 'racist-nationalist' discourse were bound to ask whether such views held back the creation of a multi-ethnic and multicultural Wales. Some of these concerns were legitimate; in particular the idea that the myth of Welsh tolerance had dampened down debates on racism in

Wales, and that Welsh-language political discourse, via the *Völkisch* idea of *gwerin*, had a part in this.[96]

Despite such insights, theories of multiculturalism that conceived of the British State as a neutral, value-free space above the petty nationalisms of its constituent peoples militated against the Welsh national project. For nationalists, the concern was that multiculturalism legitimized English as a hegemonic language in Wales, under whose umbrella smaller languages such as Welsh would be allotted a marginal role. They welcomed multi-culturalism, but wanted it to be lived through the medium of the Welsh language. Old Labour, hiding behind a façade of New Labour rhetoric, saw multiculturalism as reinforcing the role of anglophone Wales in providing a common civic culture for all. British interpretations of multiculturalism thus reinforced the belief essential to the concept of 'racist nationalism' that Welsh language campaigning was 'ethnic' and 'exclusive'.

'The warnings for a nation-building project based on language are clear', wrote Charlotte Williams. 'In many countries nationalism has incorporated racist ideology or easily slipped into erecting racialized boundaries in constructing exclusive ethnicities. [. . .] There are warnings across Europe of the construction of a New Racism built on notions of exclusive ethnicities and cultural supremacy.'[97] Speaking Welsh might force such 'exclusive' identities on black people: 'The black and ethnic-minority communities of Wales [. . .] may find a Welsh nationhood located in the Welsh language inaccessible and meaningless'.[98] Indeed 'the acquisition of the Welsh language can actually increase the invisibility of black people, and language assimilation may well have implications for their black identity.'[99] There was a linkage too between the spatial geography of Welsh-speaking communities and 'the physical territory of white Wales'.[100]

Welsh-language activists have tended to shy away from condemning such views because of a fear that criticizing ethnic minority activists would play into the hands of the 'racist-nationalist' discourse. But this makes the mistake of equating a particular viewpoint within a minority community with the minority community as a whole. Plenty of ethnic minority activists argued the other way. Welsh anti-apartheid leader Hanif Bhamjee condemned in 1995 the whole 'language-race' discourse and the 'use of racism as a weapon to attack the language and nationalism'.[101] The CRE has recently felt able to support events organized by language activists.[102] Plaid Cymru has three Muslim councillors: the highest number of any political party in Wales.

The perception that multiculturalism and the Welsh language are mutually exclusive is of course merely another constructed discourse. It depends on reading one set of evidence, the idioms of 'racist nationalism', while ignoring another, texts by language activists praising multiculturalism. 'There's no future for the Welsh language as a language spoken only by white people', argued Cymuned activist Siôn Jobbins in the group's newsletter, 'Welsh [can] develop as a lively and strong multi-ethnic language.'[103]

As multiculturalism is pitted against Welsh-language culture, the idioms of 'racist nationalism' reach their denouement, both duplicitous and irresponsible: duplicitous because they use the rhetoric of pluralism, diversity and inclusivity to degrade a minority language community; irresponsible because these manufactured idioms are heard against the background of real intolerance towards immigrants in Britain. The false 'racist-nationalist' idiom fills the space in Welsh public life that would otherwise have been used to face down real racism.

It is not wholly at odds with our analysis that such intolerance towards immigrants manifests itself among many of those who created the 'racist-nationalist' bogeyman for political expediency, and regarded the smearing of a minority culture as a price worth paying. The *Welsh Mirror* was not above directing tabloid venom at East Europeans.[104] It was the Labour party however that exhibited the most breathtaking hypocrisy. It hounded Seimon Glyn for holding the sort of views in Wales that its own politicians were espousing in England. It was in 2001 that the Labour Party started to float the idea that there should be restrictions on non-English speakers gaining citizenship of the UK.[105] Immigrants would be required to learn English. By 2002, Home Secretary David Blunkett was calling for British Asians to 'speak English' at home.[106] Proposals which established tougher regulatory frameworks for citizenship language requirements became law as part of the 2002 Nationality, Immigration and Asylum Act.

In Wales too, there were double standards. After a leaflet was distributed in Cardiff during the 2004 local election campaign that played on prejudice against Travellers and Gypsies, Labour became the only political party in early twenty-first-century Wales that had to apologize for using racist propaganda in an election campaign.[107]

Labour's xenophobia did not however enter the discourse of political racism in Wales whereas manufactured examples of 'racist nationalism' were replayed in the media again and again. Double standards were present, too, in Labour's analysis of what constituted a 'racist' idiom. When David Blunkett told a Home Office anti-racism meeting in 2003 that 'Colin Jackson succeeded, despite being Welsh', Rhodri Morgan's response was 'let him or her who has never made a slip of the tongue, cast the first stone', a courtesy not extended by Labour to language activists.[108] In the Labour never-never land of racist idiom, it appears that what makes a derogatory ethnic statement racist is an almost Calvinistic notion of ideological predestination. The nationalist is a closet racist, even before speaking, while the Labour cabinet minister is an internationalist, for whom ethnic comments can only ever be harmless banter, and language laws the product of common sense.

Patrick McGuinness makes the point that all cultures of necessity contain moments of intolerance or ethnocentricity; yet in Wales only the minority Welsh-language culture is held to account. When mainstream British political culture felt free in 2001–3 to attack asylum seekers, and discuss nationality and citizenship in exclusive and indeed 'racist' terms, the minority culture was not afforded the privilege of its own occasional moments of failing.[109] This is not to say that language activism is a perfect discourse. Language activists are only human, and like everyone else they will make mistakes, strategic errors and political *faux pas*. They will at times be insensitive, arrogant and take on themselves the mantle of righteousness. Language activism in 2001 threw up one metaphor that could be read at the level of biological racism. However, one metaphor doesn't make an idiom. The collection of disparate and often banal comments cobbled together by the *Welsh Mirror* and the Labour party in 2001 to create a narrative of 'racist nationalism' does not of itself constitute a priori evidence of a racist discourse.

It is more sensible to view the 'racist-nationalist' bogeyman as a preconceived idiom, constructed in response to a perceived political crisis in Unionist ranks – that of a nationalist breakthrough in the South Wales valleys in the 1999 first Assembly elections. In January 2001, Seimon Glyn strayed into the Labour Party's field of vision, and became the dubious example on whom that party would build its case. Electorally, the Labour Party's strategy was successful. The second Assembly elections of 2003 saw a significant fall off in support for Plaid Cymru. There was rancour within the national movement between those who wished to respond to the Seimon Glyn affair by passing by, and those, like Cymuned, who wished to challenge the 'racist-nationalist' narrative and expose it as a myth.

To be branded as racist is to have one's discourse delegitimized. It is to be silenced, indeed to be denied the right to speak. For any community such a situation is intolerable; for a minority community, it is particularly so. To leave the 'racist-nationalist' idiom intact and unchallenged is to handicap, perhaps fatally, language activism as a serious lobby in Welsh politics. If the advocates of a minority-language community are judged to be racist, their opinions will be removed from public discourse and their cause dismissed from the political agenda.

A preliminary task for those who wish to reverse this situation is to understand better how the 'racist-nationalist' bogeyman myth was constructed. This idiom has been with us since the 1930s, poisoning Welsh political and cultural life. It is hard to see how the future of the Welsh language can be constructively and openly debated until its bluff is called.

NOTES

[1] Patrick McGuinness, '"Racism" in Welsh Politics', *Planet*, 159 (June/July 2003), 7, 9, 10.

[2] See Joshua A. Fishman, *Reversing Language Shift* (Clevedon, 1991).

[3] Glyn Williams and Delyth Morris, *Language Planning and Language Use: Welsh in a Global Age* (Cardiff, 2000), 33, 35.

[4] Biographies of Assembly Members in various political publications suggest that about a quarter of AMs are English-born, a figure slightly higher than the 20.3% of the Welsh population born in England.

[5] Two of Plaid Cymru's 12 AMs were born in England. Cymuned itself was led for two years by the English-born author of this essay, and several members of its National Executive were English.

[6] Neil Evans, 'Immigrants and Minorities in Wales, 1840-1990: A Comparative Perspective', in Charlotte Williams, Neil Evans and Paul O' Leary (eds.), *A Tolerant Nation? Exploring ethnic diversity in Wales* (Cardiff, 2003), 30.

[7] 'Race-hate charge for teen's abusive attack', *Daily Post*, 4 November 2003.

[8] See, for example, Simon Brooks, '"Yr Hil": ydy'r canu caeth diweddar yn hiliol?' in Owen Thomas (ed.), *Llenyddiaeth mewn Theori* (Caerdydd, 2006), forthcoming. In a study of the word *hil* ('race') in Welsh-language strict-metre poetry since the 1970s, I conclude that it was a signifier of conservative and essentialist thought. It was not, however, racist, at least in any biological or radicalized sense.

[9] Lyn Lewis Dafis, 'Hiliaeth y Cymry', *Barn*, 488 (September 2003), 27.

[10] For these arguments, see Glyn Williams and Delyth Morris, *Language Planning and Language Use: Welsh in a Global Age*, *op. cit.*, xviii-xix; Simon Brooks, *O Dan Lygaid y Gestapo: Yr Oleuedigaeth Gymraeg a Theori Lenyddol yng Nghymru* (Caerdydd, 2004), 1-37, 113-15; Carwyn Fowler, 'Nationalism and the Labour Party in Wales', *Llafur*, 8, 4 (2003), 99–100.

[11] Gwilym Davies, 'Cymru Gyfan a'r Blaid Genedlaethol Gymreig,' *Y Traethodydd*, July 1942, quoted in T. Robin Chapman, *W Ambrose Bebb* (Caerdydd, 1997), 132.

[12] See, for example, 'Nazi Ideology of Plaid Cymru – Mr James Griffiths', *Western Mail*, 6 January 1950, quoted in Richard Wyn Jones, *Rhoi Cymru'n Gyntaf: Syniadaeth Wleidyddol Plaid Cymru*, forthcoming; T. J. Morgan quoted in Simon Brooks, *O Dan Lygaid y Gestapo: Yr Oleuedigaeth Gymraeg a Theori Lenyddol yng Nghymru, op. cit.*, 67-9.

[13] Merlyn Rees MP and Ivor Richard MP quoted in Rhys Evans, *Gwynfor: Rhag Pob Brad* (Talybont, 2005), 294.

[14] Leo Abse quoted in 'Abse predicts bilingual elite after devolution', *Western Mail*, 29 September 1978.

[15] See, for example, Paul Starling, 'Time to go back to the future, Tony', *Welsh Mirror*, 21 July 2000.

[16] Debate on 'Racism (Welsh Politics)', Hansard, 7 May 2002.

[17] Richard Wyn Jones, *Rhoi Cymru'n Gyntaf: Syniadaeth Wleidyddol Plaid Cymru*, forthcoming.

[18] Saunders Lewis quoted in *Western Mail and South Wales News*, 1 March 1934: 'the Nationalist Party must take sides with the popular masses of Wales against Fascist dictatorship'. Quoted in Richard Wyn Jones, *Rhoi Cymru'n Gyntaf: Syniadaeth Wleidyddol Plaid Cymru*, forthcoming.

[19] Richard Wyn Jones, *ibid*.

[20] Viscount Tonypandy, '"Apartheid" for Welsh speakers', letter in *The Times*, 5 September 1990.

[21] Interview with Kim Howells, 11 September 1995, BBC Scotland. Quoted in Richard Wyn Jones, *Rhoi Cymru'n Gyntaf: Syniadaeth Wleidyddol Plaid Cymru*, forthcoming.

[22] Dyddiadur Daniel, *Baner ac Amserau Cymru*, 2 May 1968. I'm grateful to Robin Chapman for this reference.

[23] Charlotte Williams, 'Claiming the National: Nation, National Identity and Ethnic Minorities', *A Tolerant Nation? Exploring ethnic diversity in Wales, op. cit.*, 224.

[24] 'Taflen yn codi gwrychyn cynghorwyr Gwynedd', *Yr Herald*, 23 November 1976.

[25] 'Comment', *North Wales Chronicle*, 4 November 1982.

[26] Ivor Wynne Jones, 'Fixing the Race', *Daily Post*, 31 October 1987; 'Racism lurks in Welsh Wales', *Daily Post*, 6 September 1988.

[27] 'I won't sell to English!', *Wales on Sunday*, 19 March 1989; Clive Betts, 'One way out of race issue', *Western Mail*, 3 May 1995.

[28] 'Y Gymraeg yn angenrheidiol', *Y Cymro*, 24 July 1979.

[29] Dafydd Wigley quoted in 'Equality vendetta against Welsh language alleged', *Western Mail*, 26 July 1985.

[30] 'Council Workers fear Welsh language edict', *The Times*, 22 September 1995; 'Clash with race board', *Daily Post*, 23 September 1995.

[31] 'Discrimination ruling on non-Welsh-speakers defended', *Western Mail*, 15 August 1985.

[32] 'Commission on "racism" charge', *Daily Post*, 11 July 2001, 7; Simon Brooks, 'Colofn Fisol y Golygydd: Hiliaeth Sefydliadol', *Barn*, 459 (April 2001), 6–7.

[33] Paul Starling, 'Let's make our nation truly united', *Welsh Mirror*, 10 July 1999.

[34] Paul Starling, 'A family affair with no elitists', *Welsh Mirror*, 18 February 2000; Paul Starling, 'Wriggling Wigley's the prince of Wales', *Welsh Mirror*, 12 May 2000; 'The Welsh Timebomb: Humphreys hits out at anti-English "fascists"', *Welsh Mirror*, 21 August 2000.

[35] Paul Starling, 'Time to Oust the Spoilers', *Welsh Mirror*, 22 September 2000.

[36] Alun Michael, 'The face behind the mask of Plaid Cymru', *Welsh Mirror*, 20 September 1999.

[37] Interview with Seimon Glyn, Sarah Dickins programme, BBC Radio Wales, 17 January 2001. Transcript verified with original interview held at the National Screen and Sound Archive of Wales.

[38] Delyth Morris, 'Geiriau Seimon', *Barn*, 462/563 (July/August 2001), 30–39.

[39] 'Police clear Seimon Glyn', *Daily Post*, 3 September 2001.

[40] 'Voice of Hate: "Racist" Plaid councillor's attack on the English', *Welsh Mirror*, 18 January 2001.

[41] 'Comments of Mr Seimon Glynn [sic]', Early Day Motion 229, House of Commons, 2001.

[42] 'Welsh Affairs', Hansard, 5th March 2001.

[43] 'Still plenty to do for better Wales: Tony Blair exclusive', *Welsh Mirror*, 2 March 2001.

[44] See, for example, Paul Starling, 'It's time to own up or resign, Mr Wyn Jones', *Welsh Mirror*, February 23 2001.

[45] '"English out" row stoked by Plaid top boss', *Welsh Mirror*, 8 August 2001.

[46] 'Councillor carpeted for anti-English "rape" speech', *Western Mail*, 17 March 2001.

47 'Plaid War of Hate', *Welsh Mirror*, 24 May 2001.

48 'Plaid Dismiss "Nazi" link', *Welsh Mirror*, 22 May 2001.

49 'Quit Row', *Welsh Mirror*, 20 August 2001.

50 Heini Gruffudd, 'Heini yr Hiliwr', *Barn*, 459 (April 2001), 17–19; Betsan Powys, 'Y Cymry Hiliol', *Barn*, 459 (April 2001), 20–24.

51 Patrick McGuinness, '"Racism" in Welsh Politics', *art. cit.*, 9.

52 John Elfed Jones, 'Buches a Buchedd', *Barn*, 462/462 (July/August 2001), 59.

53 Beca Brown, 'O ba beth y gwnaethpwyd hiliaeth?', *Barn*, 462/463 (July/August 2001), 75.

54 'TV Personality Beca turns up the heat in English Immigration Row: Yes, I'm a Racist', *Wales on Sunday*, 26 August 2001.

55 Paul Flynn, 'Gwleidyddiaeth Dabloid', *Barn*, 464 (September 2001), 14.

56 In an editorial in *Barn* in March 2002, I had talked of civil disobedience (*'anufudd-dod sifil'*). When the Labour Party released a translation of my text via press release, this term had been changed to 'civil disorder'. See News Wales website, http://www.newswales.co.uk/?section=Politics&F=5532 (seen 2 March 2006).

57 'Biased Broadcast Channel: Station accused of being "pro-nationalist"', *Welsh Daily Mirror*, 20 June 2002; Debate on 'Racism (Welsh Politics)', Hansard, 7 May 2002.

58 'A Period of De-stabilisation [:] Monitoring [:] The National Assembly for Wales [:] May to August 2001', *Nations and Regions: The Dynamics of Devolution: Quarterly Monitoring Programme Wales Quarterly Report* ed. John Osmond, August 2001, web version http://www.ucl.ac.uk/constitution-unit/monrep/wales/waaug001.pdf (seen 2 March 2006).

59 Statement signed by 48 academics at the University of Wales, 'Yn erbyn y Sensor', *Barn*, 462/463 (July/August 2001), 49.

60 'Race Row Begun "on purpose"', *Welsh Mirror*, 22 February 2001.

61 See, for example, letter from Chris Ruane MP to Wyn Hobson of Cymuned, 4 September 2002; Martyn Jones MP, letter to Wyn Hobson, 21 May 2002.

62 'Language of Hatred: Welsh group faces Home Office racism probe', *Welsh Mirror*, 7 November 2001.

63 'Graffiti Policy for Gwynedd' [Gwynedd County Council policy document], 10 February 2004, point 1.4 and 2.5 http://www.gwynedd.gov.uk/upload/public/attachments/268/EITEM_6.doc (seen 2 March 2006). Graffiti was defined under the policy to include any poster or advert in contravention of planning regulations.

64 Siôn Jobbins, 'Dreyfus Cymru a'r Wlad Newydd', *Barn*, 467/468 (December/January 2001/2), 36.

65 Richard Wyn Jones, 'Barn ar Gymru: Normal Business will be resuming shortly', *Barn*, 471 (April 2002), 10.

66 Patrick McGuinness, 'The War on Welsh: An Update', *Planet*, 155 (October/November 2002), 59; Patrick McGuinness, 'Reflections in the "Welsh" Mirror', *Planet* 153 (June/July 2002), 10.

67 Paul Starling, 'Broken English demand', *Welsh Mirror*, 31 July 1999; Paul Starling, 'Our country won't make it all alone', *Welsh Mirror*, July 13 2001; Paul Starling, 'Stand Up and be Counted', *Welsh Mirror*, August 24 2001; 'Welsh Apartheid', *Welsh Mirror*, 15 June 2001; Paul Starling, 'It's time to own up or resign, Mr Wyn Jones', *art. cit.*

68 Paul Starling, 'Hate mail delivers no sense', *Welsh Mirror*, 27 July 2001; Paul Starling, 'Flush out Fascists', *Welsh Mirror*, 15 June 2001; Paul Starling,

'Welsh politics? That's kids' stuff', *Welsh Mirror*, 21 December 2001; Paul Starling, 'Plaid face D-day', *Welsh Mirror*, 23 November 2001.

[69] 'Racist Terrorists', *Welsh Daily Mirror*, 12 July 2002; Paul Starling, 'Pride in Hero's Letter', *Welsh Mirror*, July 27 2001; Paul Starling, 'S4C mission fails', *Welsh Mirror*, November 9 2001.

[70] Paul Starling, 'Evil bigots choking the life out of Wales', *Welsh Daily Mirror*, 12 July 2002; Paul Starling, '2003: The year of big decisions', *Welsh Daily Mirror*, January 3 2003.

[71] Paul Starling, 'Bigots Harm Wales', *Welsh Mirror*, June 22 2001; Paul Starling, 'Starling: Rhodri comes back to earth', *Welsh Daily Mirror*, November 15 2002.

[72] Paul Starling, 'Time for Festival of Fear and Hatred', *Welsh Daily Mirror*, August 2 2002.

[73] Charlotte Williams, 'Strange Encounters', *Planet*, 158 (April/May 2003), 21.

[74] Patrick McGuinness, 'The War on Welsh: An Update', *art. cit.*, 58.

[75] Paul Starling quoted in ibid., 59.

[76] Tim Saunders, 'Y Gelyn Mewnol', *Barn*, 474/475 (July/August 2002), 20.

[77] Paul Starling, 'Don't be fooled by magic circle', *Welsh Mirror*, November 23 2001; Paul Starling, 'Time for Festival of Fear and Hatred', *art. cit.*

[78] Paul Starling, 'Bigots Harm Wales', *art. cit.*

[79] Patrick McGuinness, 'Single Issues and Double Standards', *Planet*, 166 (August/September 2004), 14–15.

[80] Cartoon in *Welsh Daily Mirror*, 12 July 2002.

[81] See, for example, David Denney, 'The Social Construction of Nationalism: Racism and Conflict in Wales', *Contemporary Wales*, 4 (1991), 150-165; David Denney, John Borland and Ralph Fevre, 'Nation, Community and Conflict: Housing Policy and Immigration in North Wales', *National, Identity and Social Theory: Perspectives from Wales* (ed. Ralph Fevre and Andrew Thompson) (Cardiff, 1999), 129–148.

[82] Beca Brown quoted in Charlotte Williams, 'Strange Encounters', *art. cit.*, 158.

[83] Charlotte Williams, 'Social Inclusion and Race Equality in Wales', *A Tolerant Nation? Exploring ethnic diversity in Wales*, *op. cit.*, 144, 'Claiming the National: Nation, National Identity and Ethnic Minorities', *A Tolerant Nation? Exploring ethnic diversity in Wales*, *op. cit.*, 223, 225.

[84] See, for example, Bernard Levin, 'A pantomime dragon, but its venom will surely kill', *The Times*, 30 August 1990; Stephen Pollard, 'Waste of Money, so to speak', *The Express*, 7 August 1998.

[85] Robert Kilroy Silk, 'Hills are alive to the sound of racism', *Daily Express* quoted in 'Rhagfarnau'r Wasg Seisnig', *Yr Herald*, 7 May 1994.

[86] 'Inside the ranks of police racism', *The Observer*, 26 October 2003 on *Observer* website http://observer.guardian.co.uk/uk_news/story/0,6903,1071220,00.html (seen 1 March 2006).

[87] Abigail Hole, Etain O' Carroll, John King, *Lonely Planet: Wales* (London, 2004), 37.

[88] 'Talk: Plaid Cymru', http://en.wikipedia.org/wiki/Talk:Plaid_Cymru (seen 17 March 2006).

[89] See Edward Said, *Orientalism: Western Conceptions of the Orient* (London, 1978).

[90] Glyn Williams, 'Discourses on "Nation" and "Race": A Response to Denney *et al.*', *Contemporary Wales*, 6 (1994), 93.

[91] 'Cymuned activists "as bad as the far right"', *Daily Post*, 4 May 2002.

[92] Richard Wyn Jones, 'Barn ar Gymru: Brwydr Fudr', *Barn*, 477 (October 2002), 13.

[93] During Labour's 2001 Welsh Conference, speakers juxtaposed condemnation of supposed Welsh language 'monoculturalism' with the 'diversity' of the 'hundred' or so languages spoken in Swansea: the subtext, of course, being that Welsh language rights somehow undermined ethnic minority languages.

[94] Don Touhig, 'Written Response to the Western Mail', 1 September 2003 on www.dontouhig.org.uk/lewis.htm (seen 6 October 2005).

[95] 'Storm over English race claim', BBC News website, 8 August 2003, http://news.bbc.co.uk/2/hi/uk_news/wales/3134383.stm (seen 17 March 2006).

[96] See, for example, Charlotte Williams, '"Race and Racism: What's Special about Wales?' in David Dunkerley and Andrew Thompson (eds.), *Wales Today* (Cardiff, 1999), 277.

[97] Charlotte Williams, '"Race" and Racism: Some Reflections on the Welsh Context', *Contemporary Wales*, 8 (1995), 126. See also, Charlotte Williams, 'Passports to Wales? Race, Nation and Identity', *National, Identity and Social Theory: Perspectives from Wales*, *op. cit.*, 73.

[98] Charlotte Williams, 'Passports to Wales? Race, Nation and Identity', *National, Identity and Social Theory: Perspectives from Wales*, *op. cit.*, 86.

[99] Charlotte Williams, '"Race" and Racism: Some Reflections on the Welsh Context', *art. cit.*, 124.

[100] Charlotte Williams, 'Passports to Wales? Race, Nation and Identity', *National, Identity and Social Theory: Perspectives from Wales*, op. cit., 75.

[101] Hanif Bhamjee quoted in 'Iaith a *hil*iaith', *Y Cymro*, 11 October 1995 and in 'Comisiwn Hiliol yn syrthio ar ei fai', *Y Cymro*, 22 November 1995.

[102] The CRE subcontracted the arrangement of a public consultation meeting in North Wales on the Commission's draft housing policy to Cymuned in 2005, and invited Cymuned to be a partner in their 2006 'Croeso' programme. Chris Myant, CRE Director in Wales, also spoke at a Cymdeithas yr Iaith 'Welsh – Equal Rights?' lobby in the National Assembly in 2006.

[103] Siôn Jobbins, 'Croeso i'r Comisiwn', *Newyddion y Fro* [Cymuned newsletter], 12, February 2006, 2. 'Nid oes dyfodol i'r Gymraeg os bydd yn iaith sy'n cael ei siarad gan bobl wyn yn unig. [. . .] Dim ond polisiau cadarn Cymuned gall sicrhau fod y Gymraeg yn datblygu'n iaith aml-ethnig fywiog a chryf [. . .].'

[104] See, for example, 'Send Home Drug Scum: Kick Out Albanians warns Wales chief constable', *Welsh Daily Mirror*, 7 February 2003.

[105] 'Immigrants face new language rule', BBC News website, 19 August 2001, http://news.bbc.co.uk/1/hi/uk_politics/1498091.stm (seen 27 February 2006).

[106] 'PM backs Blunkett in Race Row', BBC News website, 16 September 2002, http://news.bbc.co.uk/1/hi/uk_politics/2254666.stm (seen 27 February 2006).

[107] 'Welsh Labour apologise for offensive leaflet', CRE website, 29 September 2004, http://www.cre.gov.uk/Default.aspx.LocID-0hgnew00o.RefLocID-0hg00900c001002.Lang-EN.htm (seen 1 March 2006).

[108] 'Outrage at Blunkett's "stupid" Welsh jibe', *Western Mail*, 15 January 2003.

[109] Patrick McGuinness, '"Racism" in Welsh Politics', *art. cit.*, 12.

Notes on Contributors

Ursula Masson lectures in History at the University of Glamorgan and is, among other things, chair of Archif Menywod Cymru/ Women's Archive of Wales.

T. Robin Chapman is a lecturer in Welsh at University of Wales, Aberystwyth.

Damian Walford Davies is a senior lecturer in English at University of Wales, Aberystwyth.

Emily Charette is a postdoctoral researcher in the Department of International Politics, University of Wales, Aberystwyth.

Nick Bourne is leader of the Welsh Conservatives in the National Assemby Government.

Avril Rolph works in Library and Information Services at University of Wales, Swansea.

Simon Brooks is editor of the Welsh current affairs magazine *Barn* and an honorary research fellow in the Department of Welsh, University of Wales, Lampeter.